CURRY LEAVES
AND CUMIN SEEDS

JEETI GANDHI

PHOTOGRAPHY BY **DIRK PIETERS**

FOOD STYLING BY **ABIGAIL DONNELLY**

Struik Publishers
(a division of New Holland Publishing
(South Africa) (Pty) Ltd)
Cornelis Struik House
80 McKenzie Street
Cape Town 8001
South Africa
www.struik.co.za
New Holland Publishing is a member
of the Johnnic Publishing Group

First published in 2002
1 2 3 4 5 6 7 8 9 10

Publishing manager: Linda de Villiers
Managing editor: Cecilia Barfield
Editor: Catherine Murray
Designer: Petal Palmer
Assistant designers: Sean Robertson and Beverley Dodd
Photographer: Dirk Pieters
Food stylist: Abigail Donnelly
Proofreader and indexer: Pat Barton
Reproduction: Hirt & Carter Cape (Pty) Ltd
Printing and binding: Craft Print PTE Ltd, Singapore

ISBN 1 86872 627 4

With thanks to the following for
supplying props:
LIM, L'Orangerie, Moroccan
Warehouse, Loft Living, Pieter Visser
Interiors, Block & Chisel Interiors,
Summer House and Plush Bazaar

CONTENTS

INTRODUCTION

A few months ago, at an elite social gathering in Johannesburg, I overheard a discussion on Indian cuisine. Some of the comments made are still vivid in my memory. One of the ladies said, 'To make any dish taste Indian, I just add curry.' 'But curry is so hot and spicy, I never enjoy eating it,' another replied. Then someone else complained that although she loved Indian curry, it was too rich and oily for her liking. Yet another, who seemed to enjoy cooking, said that her family loved Indian food and she would love to cook it at home, but she was put off by the fact that it seemed so time consuming and it was her impression that not all the spices were readily available. Though I was happy to hear that people loved Indian cuisine, I couldn't help feeling that most of the comments I'd overheard were sadly unjustified.

On another occasion I hosted a large dinner party, to which several African friends and business associates were invited. From starters to dessert, every dish was Indian. For convenience I labelled each dish with its name and a brief description of the ingredients. When dinner was served, I noticed that most guests served very little of each dish on their plates (perhaps they didn't know what to expect). However, within the next few minutes I noticed some of them returning to the table for seconds, with very flattering comments like 'I have never tasted anything so delicious and full of flavour', 'You don't get food like this in Indian restaurants', 'Would you mind giving me some of these recipes?', and 'Are all the spices you need available here, or do you get them from India?'.

That evening so encouraged me that I decided to compile a cookery book full of delicious and easy-to-prepare Indian recipes, along with basic information about Indian food and traditions, for my friends in South Africa who enjoy Indian cuisine and would like to cook it at home.

I have also been inspired by a South African friend who, despite a strict vegetarian diet, has enjoyed many nutritious, well-balanced vegetarian meals at my home. Worldwide, more and more people are turning vegetarian, either on medical advice or by choice. A common complaint is that vegetarian food can become monotonous, and it is difficult to find recipes with the right nutritional balance, particularly of protein. This book should fill that gap by providing plenty of nutritious and delicious vegetarian recipes.

Indian cuisine is a unique combination of different spices and herbs with meat, fish, seafood, vegetables, lentils, pulses, dry beans and peas, paneer (home-made fresh cheese) and yoghurt. Certain recipes require one or two spices only, while more elaborate ones may need eight to ten or more spices to obtain the desired flavour. It is therefore correct to say that Indian food is 'spicy', but not always 'hot' or 'pungent'. The only spice that makes Indian food hot is green or red chillies, chopped or in powdered form. These can either be totally eliminated or the amount adjusted according to taste without affecting the flavour of the dish. The amount of other spices used in the recipes can also be altered according to taste. If you prefer a pungent taste, add extra green chilli or hot chilli powder.

Do not be put off by long lists of ingredients. Once you have the recommended list of spices on your shelf, along with any others required by the recipe, every dish will be simple to prepare and delicious to eat.

As I come from north India, most of the recipes in this book are from that region and a special effort has been made to avoid the use of unhealthy ingredients. Ghee, cream and butter are either used sparingly or are replaced by unsaturated vegetable oil as the cooking medium.

So go ahead and try some of my recipes, and surprise your family or friends with a delicious, home-cooked Indian meal. I can assure you that, without exception, they will taste far better than the so-called Indian food made with 'curry powder'!

FROM LEFT TO RIGHT: TURMERIC, GREEN CHILLIES, CORIANDER, BABY EGGPLANT

Regional and cultural differences in Indian cuisine

Religion has a great influence on the food habits of Indians. Hinduism has been the predominant religion for centuries, and most high-caste Hindus do not eat meat, fish or poultry. There are those who may eat only fish. Beef is strictly forbidden for religious reasons. Cow slaughter in certain states of India is prohibited as Hindus consider the cow a sacred animal and a great provider. People from other faiths, such as Muslims, may eat all types of meat except pork, while Christians have no such prohibitions.

India is a vast country that is divided into many states and different territories. Apart from the geographical and regional divides, there are, as mentioned above, the religious and cultural differences. There are numerous languages and dialects spoken and almost every region has its own culinary tradition and style. A north Indian meal will be totally different from a typical south Indian meal, for example. The Mughal invasion of India during the sixteenth century had a great impact on food habits, particularly in the northern Indian states. Hence northern cuisine, including Mughlai specialities, are strongly influenced by central Asian cuisine. North Indians love rich food and tend to use more cream, ghee (clarified butter) and nuts in cooking, a trend which is of course changing as people become increasingly health conscious. They prefer to grind their spices and prepare different masalas (spice mixes) at home.

Coastal states in the east have an abundance of fish, and consequently fish is preferred over other meats. The cooking medium is mustard oil, whereas in the western and southern coastal regions more coconut and coconut oil are used in cooking. The use of tamarind juice to impart a subtle, sour taste to various dishes is also common.

In Rajasthan and part of Gujarat (desert areas) a great variety of legumes, dehydrated vegetables and preserves like vegetable pickles are used in cooking owing to the non-availability of many fresh vegetables.

The only common factor linking these diverse cookery traditions is the use of spices to create endless aromas and flavours typical of the Indian kitchen.

How to serve and eat Indian food

Traditionally, Indians eat three main meals, breakfast, lunch and dinner, as well as afternoon tea (very British). In some communities, breakfast and lunch are combined (brunch), followed by a light snack in the afternoon and then dinner.

A typical Indian meal consists of a dish with gravy (to you, 'curry') be it meat or fish for non-vegetarians, or dried peas, beans or daal (pulses, including lentils), or paneer (home-made cheese) for vegetarians. In addition a vegetable dish, plain yoghurt or raita (yoghurt with vegetables such as cucumber, spinach, tomatoes), rice or chapati (Indian bread made with wholewheat flour) or both, some chopped-up salad with lime juice dressing or green chutney and pickle.

FROM LEFT TO RIGHT: WHOLE CLOVES AND WHOLE NUTMEG, SAFFRON, STAR ANISE, GROUND MASALA

GROUND DRIED CHILLIES

Generally, there aren't different courses in an Indian meal as in the western world, with the exception of dessert or Indian sweetmeats, which may be served separately after the meal. Some snacks, which may be served with tea in the afternoon, and often many other Indian dishes are not confined to a particular meal and can be served with lunch, dinner or simply as a snack. This, however, is changing and people like to serve some snacks with cocktails or starters before a meal when entertaining.

Traditionally, food is served in steel, silver or other metal plates called thalis. Small metal bowls – katories – are placed in a thali for yoghurt preparations and wet dishes. Cooked food is usually placed in serving bowls on the dining table. Everyone then serves their food into their individual thalis and katories. Alternatively, food is served in individual thalis from the kitchen and brought to the table, a tradition still followed by many orthodox Indian families. Diners may be seated on the floor on mats or rugs and the thalis placed in front of them on individual low tables. Many serve food on banana leaves and in plates and bowls made with banian leaves. This practice is most prevalent during religious ceremonies and marriages, especially in southern India.

Garnishes are simple, such as chopped fresh dhania (fresh coriander leaves), onion rings or slices, green chillies, lemon slices or wedges. Curd (yoghurt) preparations are garnished with chilli powder, black pepper or cumin powder.

Food is usually eaten with the fingers. A small piece of chapati is broken and wrapped around some meat or vegetable, and then eaten. Even rice is usually mixed with wet dishes or yoghurt and neatly eaten with the fingers. With western influence, however, the old traditions are disappearing and more and more people these days are using crockery and cutlery (mainly spoons).

I have provided serving suggestions with most of the recipes to help you to prepare a typical Indian meal for your family or when entertaining. Feel free to mix and match east with west. Serve an Indian dry vegetable dish with roasted or grilled meat or fish. Eat bread or bread rolls with Indian meat dishes instead of chapati or rice. Serve vegetable, meat or rice pulao with a tossed salad or plain yoghurt, and so on. Be adventurous and try as many dishes as possible!

Useful tips to make life easier

Preparing some of the most frequently used ingredients in Indian dishes can be very discouraging. If you would really like to enjoy Indian meals more often and save time and energy, I have a few suggestions to make that have proved very helpful to me, especially when I did not have any domestic help.

The most important tip is first to read the recipe carefully and make sure you have all the ingredients in stock. Prior to starting actual cooking, measure out and prepare the ingredients according to the instructions, and only then start to cook.

Onions, garlic and ginger

In most recipes, these three ingredients are frequently used. To process them every time you want to cook an Indian dish is time-consuming. I therefore do the following:

Onions

As and when time permits, grind extra onions in the food processor and brown them in oil. If the fat content is a consideration, use the least quantity of oil and add a little water to prevent the onions from burning, and stir frequently. Heat the oil over high heat in a non-stick pan. Add onions and reduce heat slightly. Fry, stirring occasionally, until golden brown. Cool, then divide into portions (depending on the recipes you want to try in future), place in small containers or small plastic bags and freeze. This preparation is suitable for dishes with gravy. Remember the appearance and texture of anything with gravy will depend on how well the onions are browned.

Similarly, finely chopped onions can be sautéed and frozen for making dry vegetable balti preparations and legume dishes.

Garlic and ginger

These ingredients are available in paste form in most supermarkets. Personally, I prefer to make my own as the flavour of freshly prepared paste is far superior – even after freezing – and it contains no preservatives.

I buy 200 g of each and soak them separately in sufficient water for at least 4–5 hours or preferably overnight, as this makes peeling much easier. Grind them separately in the food processor to a smooth paste. Use a few drops of water if necessary. Cut kitchen foil into 8 x 8 cm pieces. Drop 1 t (5 ml) of garlic or ginger paste onto each piece and fold it into a small parcel. Place them all in a box or freezer bag, label and freeze.

Defrost the quantity you require as and when you need it.

Masala

Preparing your masala (p 122) in advance will save you from having to do all the preparations at once.

Fresh coriander (dhania/cilantro)

In the preparation of Indian cuisine, there is no substitute for fresh coriander. It is readily available in most supermarkets, I am happy to say. Unfortunately it does not stay fresh for very long. To make sure I always have it available, I buy an extra quantity, wash it, cut off the roots, chop it up finely and freeze it in an airtight container. It is not necessary to thaw it before using.

Paneer

Paneer is a most versatile ingredient and can be prepared in a variety of ways, in a short time. I always make paneer (p 119) using at least 5 litres of milk, and freeze it. Freezing does not affect the quality or the taste. Just cut paneer into small cubes and place in two or three freezing bags and freeze.

Cooking extra quantities

A useful time and effort saver is to cook an extra quantity of your favourite dishes and freeze them for later use. Most Indian dishes can be frozen for months without losing their flavour. Potato is the only exception, as it does not freeze well. Any frozen Indian food should be thawed completely before re-heating.

Approximate equivalents

When dealing with food in the kitchen, I find it rather difficult to work with very precise weights and measures. Slight inaccuracy in conversion (see below) sometimes occurs and is permissible, if it is close to the actual. Keep a set of standard measuring spoons and measuring cups handy – they are readily available and economical to buy.

Measure	Is equal to
1 teaspoon	60 drops, 5 ml
3 teaspoons	1 tablespoon, 15 ml
4 tablespoons	¼ cup, 60 ml
16 tablespoons	1 cup, 250 ml

Abbreviations

T = tablespoon (15 ml); **t** = teaspoon (5 ml)

STARTERS

The concept of serving appetisers in Indian homes is a comparatively

recent trend, borrowed from the western world. Nowadays it is an

integral part of Indian cuisine and all sorts of snacks are served with

cocktails or as a starter before a meal.

Most of the recipes in this section can also be served as

accompaniments to main dishes, as a snack between meals, or as a

light meal. Served as a snack between meals, the dishes will obviously

go further than if they were served as starters.

The tandoori dishes in the following chapter may also be served as

starters, particularly the kebabs.

AND SNACKS

ALOO CHAAT
POTATO CANAPES

MAKES 12 PIECES

2 medium potatoes, peeled, cooked
and cut into very small cubes
½ cup (125 ml) bean sprouts
(chopped if shoots are long)
1 T (15 ml) finely chopped onion
1 T (15 ml) chopped fresh coriander
1 green chilli, finely chopped (optional)
1½ t (7.5 ml) ground cumin

½ t (2.5 ml) black salt (optional)
½ t (2.5 ml) pepper
½ t (2.5 ml) chilli powder (optional)
1 t (5 ml) castor sugar (optional)
3 T (45 ml) lemon juice
12 slices cucumber, 1 cm thick, with peel
mint sprigs, for garnish

In a bowl, mix together the potatoes, bean sprouts, onion, coriander and chilli. In another small bowl place all the dry spices, sugar if desired and lemon juice and mix thoroughly. Add to vegetables and toss well. Adjust seasoning to taste. Place cucumber slices on a platter, top each with a spoonful of chaat and garnish with a mint sprig.

TIP
Can be prepared in advance. Cover with clingfilm and refrigerate until required.

CHANA BHAJIA
FRIED CHICKPEA SAVOURIES

SERVES 12

1 x 410 g tin chickpeas
1 egg
¼ cup (60 ml) flour
½ t (2.5 ml) cumin seeds
1 t (5 ml) ground cumin
½ t (2.5 ml) chilli powder
salt to taste

½ t (2.5 ml) baking powder
2 T (30 ml) finely chopped onion
1 t (5 ml) ginger paste
1 green chilli, seeded and finely chopped (optional)
3 T (45 ml) finely chopped fresh coriander
oil for deep frying

Drain the chickpeas in a sieve and rinse briefly under running tap water. Place the chickpeas, egg and flour in a blender and blend until a slightly coarse paste forms. Add a tiny bit of water if it is too thick to blend. The consistency should be like thick cake batter. Pour into a mixing bowl. Add the remaining ingredients, except the oil, and adjust the seasoning.

Heat enough oil to fry bhajia in batches over medium heat. Using two teaspoons, drop the batter in small amounts into the hot oil. Using a slotted spoon, turn the bhajias a few times. Fry until golden brown or until cooked through. Drain off the extra oil over paper towel.

Serve hot on toothpicks with pudina chutney (p 123) or tomato sauce for dipping.

CHANA BHAJIA

ALOO CHAAT

BAINGAN KACHRI

SPICY EGGPLANT SLICES

MAKES ABOUT 12 SLICES

1 T (15 ml) lemon juice
½ t (2.5 ml) salt
1 T (15 ml) oil
1 large eggplant, cut into 1 cm thick slices
1 T (15 ml) oil
1 medium onion, finely chopped
1 t (5 ml) finely chopped garlic
1 green chilli, seeded and finely chopped (optional)
1 T (15 ml) coriander seeds, pounded
1 T (15 ml) cumin seeds, pounded
salt to taste
1 large tomato, chopped
2 T (30 ml) chopped fresh coriander
½ t (2.5 ml) black pepper
1 t (5 ml) dry mango powder or
1 T (15 ml) lemon juice
mint leaves, for garnish
cherry tomatoes, halved, for garnish

Mix together the lemon juice, salt and 1 T (15 ml) oil. Brush on both sides of each eggplant slice. Grill until tender and light brown. Keep warm. In a non-stick frying pan, heat 1 T (15 ml) oil over medium heat. Add onion, garlic and green chilli, if using, and sauté until translucent. Add the coriander and cumin seeds and salt and sauté for a few seconds more. Stir in all the remaining ingredients and cook until the tomato is just heated through (do not overcook). Top each eggplant slice with the cooked mixture and garnish with mint leaves and cherry tomatoes.
Serve as a starter or as a side dish with any main dish of your choice, with chapati (p 98) or rice.

SABZI PAKORA

VEGETABLE FRITTERS

MAKES ABOUT 60 FRITTERS

vegetables
1 green pepper, seeded, cut vertically into
   1.5 cm-thick pieces
1 small eggplant, sliced into 7 mm-thick pieces
1 cup (250 ml) small cauliflower florets
1 medium potato, peeled and cut into thin rounds
12 small, tender leaves of spinach
12 baby corn cobs, slit in half lengthwise
oil for deep frying
batter
2 cups (500 ml) gram flour* or cake flour
½ t (2.5 ml) turmeric
½ t (2.5 ml) baking powder
½ t (2.5 ml) cumin seeds
1 t (5 ml) ground cumin
½ t (2.5 ml) chilli powder or to taste
salt to taste
1 t (5 ml) garlic paste
½ t (2.5 ml) ginger paste
water

Pat vegetables dry with kitchen towel and set aside.
   To make the batter, sift the flour into a bowl. Add all remaining ingredients except the water. Gradually add water, stirring well to make a thick batter, rather like crumpet batter.
   Heat oil in a deep pan or wok. Dip a few pieces of vegetable in the batter to coat them completely and deep fry in hot oil until golden brown. Do not fry too many pakoras at once as this will reduce the oil's temperature and make the pakoras soggy and oily. It is advisable to fry each type of vegetable in separate batches.
   Drain on kitchen paper towel. Serve hot with pudina chutney (p 123).

* In India we use gram flour (basen) for making pakoras, but plain, all-purpose flour may be used. In South Africa any Indian store will stock gram flour. It gives a very subtle flavour to this dish.

ALOO SOYA TIKKI

POTATO AND SOYA BABY BURGERS

MAKES 16 SMALL CAKES

½ cup (125 ml) dry soya granules*
2 medium potatoes, cooked and peeled
2 slices plain brown bread
2 T (30 ml) finely chopped onion
3 T (45 ml) finely chopped fresh coriander
1 t (5 ml) finely chopped root ginger
1 green chilli, seeded and finely chopped (optional)
1½ t (7.5 ml) ground cumin
1 T (15 ml) cornflour
½ t (2.5 ml) garam masala (p 122)
1 T (15 ml) lemon juice
salt to taste
oil for deep frying

Prepare the soya granules (see page 120) or follow the instructions on the label. Set aside. Chop the potatoes coarsely and place in a mixing bowl. Soak the bread slices in water and immediately squeeze dry. Crumble into the mixing bowl with the potatoes and mash with a potato masher. Add all the remaining ingredients, except the oil. Adjust the seasoning and divide the mixture into 16 equal portions. Shape into small burgers (tikkis). Heat the oil and fry 4–5 pieces at a time until golden brown. Serve hot, garnished with onion rings.
Serve with yoghurt pudina chutney (p 123) or with tomato or peri-peri sauce.

*If you are not very keen on soya granules, add 1 extra potato and ¼ cup (60 ml) each of chopped cooked beans and carrots instead.

TIP
The tikkis can be fried ahead of time. Place uncovered in a single layer in a warm oven until ready to serve. They will stay crisp. Make larger tikkis and serve with a green salad for a light lunch.

MACHHI AMRITSARI

SPICY FRIED FISH

SERVES 6

Amritsar is a city in northern India, of which this dish is a speciality.

400 g fish fillets (any firm white fish)
1 t (5 ml) ginger paste
1 t (5 ml) garlic paste
1 t (5 ml) fresh lemon juice
2 t (10 ml) tandoori masala (p 122)
½ t (2.5 ml) salt
3 T (45 ml) cake flour
3 T (45 ml) cornflour
1 t (5 ml) garam masala (p 122)
1 t (5 ml) ground cumin
½ t (2.5 ml) carum seeds (optional)
½ t (2.5 ml) pepper
½ t (2.5 ml) chilli powder or cayenne pepper
salt to taste
oil for deep frying

Cut fish into 4 x 4 cm pieces and place in a mixing bowl. Rub with ginger, garlic, lemon juice, tandoori masala and salt. Keep aside.
In a small polythene bag, mix together all the remaining ingredients, except the oil. Place 3–4 pieces of fish in the bag and shake well to coat each piece with the flour mixture. Remove the coated pieces and repeat with the remaining pieces of fish.
Heat the oil in a wok or a deep pan. Fry the fish in batches until crisp and golden in colour. Drain on kitchen paper towel and keep warm. Serve immediately.
Serve plain or with dahi pudina chutney (p 123). The fish can also be served as a main course with daal, kheera pudina raita (p 75) and rice, or with mashed potatoes and a salad of your choice.

PANEER CHAAT

PANEER CHAAT

SPICY HOME-MADE CHEESE

SERVES 8

240 g low-fat paneer cubes (2 cm each)
1 t (5 ml) ground cumin
½ t (2.5 ml) roasted ground cumin (see page 122)
1 t (5 ml) ginger juice
½ t (2.5 ml) black pepper
½ t (2.5 ml) chilli powder
2 T (30 ml) finely chopped fresh coriander
1 t (5 ml) white sugar
1 T (15 ml) lemon juice
salt to taste

Place paneer cubes in a mixing bowl. Add cumin, ginger juice, pepper and chilli powder. Set aside. Place coriander and sugar in a mortar and grind with a pestle until the sugar is crushed. Add lemon juice and salt. Stir in paneer mixture and mix gently. Serve on toothpicks on a bed of lettuce leaves.

MAKKI KE PAKORA

SPICY CORN FRITTERS

SERVES 8

2 cups (500 ml) frozen corn
2 T (30 ml) finely chopped onion
2 t (10 ml) finely chopped root ginger
1 green chilli, seeded and finely chopped (optional)
2 T (30 ml) finely chopped fresh coriander
1 t (5 ml) ground cumin
1 t (5 ml) paprika
salt to taste
1 egg, well beaten
½ t (2.5 ml) bicarbonate of soda
¾ cup (180 ml) cake flour
oil for deep frying

Place all the ingredients, except the oil in a mixing bowl and mix thoroughly. If it is too thick and dry, add a little water to get a consistency of thick paste.

Heat sufficient oil in a wok, or any other suitable pan for deep frying, over high heat until a drop of corn mixture fries quickly. Now drop the mixture by the spoonful (6–8 at a time) and fry until deep golden in colour. Remove with a slotted spoon and place on kitchen paper towel to drain.

Serve hot, with dahi pudina chutney (p 123).

There is a great variety of dishes that can be listed under this section. Different kinds of meat, fish, paneer and vegetables can be cooked tandoori style. One characteristic common to most is the use of yoghurt, ginger and garlic, though the combination of spices may differ.

Kebabs and tikkas are terms generally used for a variety of small pieces of meat cooked in a tandoor, on an open fire, grilled or fried. The most important characteristic of good kebabs or tikkas is that they should be lightly charred on the outside and succulent inside, and should almost melt in your mouth. Overcooking can spoil the flavour and make them dry and chewy.

Yoghurt marinade helps to tenderise meat to an extent, but is not enough to achieve the desired texture when it is cooked. For convenience, I generally use a commercially available meat tenderiser – unripe papaya is the best and most effective. Peel and grind it, and add to yoghurt, ginger and garlic marinade. Most kebabs and tikkas should be left to marinate for 6–8 hours, or preferably overnight. This helps to tenderise the meat so well that it requires only a little cooking. Always select prime cuts of meat for best results.

Most meats and fish with tandoori marinade can be frozen for several weeks. Bring to room temperature before cooking. Leftover marinade can be mixed with oil and used for basting during the last 5–7 minutes of grilling.

Most tandoori dishes can be served as starters or with a main meal, and the size of servings adjusted accordingly. Serving suggestions at the end of each recipe give various serving options. All types of kebabs may be used as a filling for bread rolls or pita bread.

FROM THE
OOR

MURGI KA TIKKA

CHICKEN TIKKA

SERVES 6 AS A STARTER OR 3 AS A MAIN COURSE

400 g boneless chicken, cubed
1 T (15 ml) oil, for basting
marinade
¾ cup (180 ml) low-fat yoghurt
1 t (5 ml) ginger paste
2 t (10 ml) garlic paste
2 t (10 ml) fresh lemon juice
1½ t (7.5 ml) tandoori masala (p 122)
1 t (5 ml) garam masala (p 122)
1 t (5 ml) chilli powder or to taste
salt to taste

First make the marinade by mixing together all the marinade ingredients in a bowl. Add the chicken cubes and stir through until they are thoroughly coated in marinade. Cover and marinate in the refrigerator for 5–6 hours, or preferably overnight.

Bring the marinated chicken to room temperature before cooking. Thread the chicken pieces onto skewers. Braai (barbecue) or grill, turning and basting every few minutes until cooked through, but still juicy (about 15–20 minutes).

Serve the chicken pieces on toothpicks instead of skewers, with pudina chutney (p 123) as a starter or as a main meal along with a legume dish, a vegetable dish, chapati (p 98) or rice and raita.

MURGI MALAI KABAB

CREAMY CHICKEN KEBABS

SERVES 6 AS A STARTER OR 3 AS A MAIN COURSE

400 g boneless chicken, cubed
1 T (15 ml) oil, for basting
marinade
2 T (30 ml) almond paste (p 123)
3 T (45 ml) cream
1 T (15 ml) garlic paste
2 t (10 ml) ginger paste
¼ t (1.25 ml) ground mace
¼ t (1.25 ml) grated nutmeg
½ t (2.5 ml) chilli powder or to taste
½ t (2.5 ml) pepper
2 t (10 ml) cornflour
1 T (15 ml) finely chopped fresh coriander
salt to taste

First make the marinade by mixing together all the marinade ingredients in a bowl. Add the chicken and mix well. Cover and marinate in the refrigerator for 5–6 hours, or preferably overnight.

Bring to room temperature before cooking. Thread the chicken pieces onto skewers. Braai (barbecue) or grill, turning and basting every few minutes until cooked through, but still juicy (about 15–20 minutes).

Serve the chicken pieces on toothpicks instead of skewers, with pudina chutney (p 123) as a starter or as a main meal along with a legume dish, a vegetable dish, naan (p 105) or chapati (p 98), and raita.

MURGI KA TIKKA

TANDOORI MURGI

SEEKH KABAB

TANDOORI MURGI
TANDOORI CHICKEN
SERVES 4

4 small chicken drumsticks and 4 thighs, or 4 skinless breast fillets
1 t (5 ml) chilli powder or to taste
2 T (30 ml) lemon juice
½ t (2.5 ml) salt
2 T (30 ml) oil, for basting
marinade
¾ cup (180 ml) low-fat yoghurt, whisked
2 t (10 ml) ginger paste
1 T (15 ml) garlic paste
1 t (5 ml) garam masala (p 122)
1½ t (7.5 ml) tandoori masala (p 122)
salt to taste

Separate the drumsticks from the thighs or cut each breast into two pieces. With a sharp knife, make 2–3 deep slits on both sides of each piece. Set aside.
Mix together the chilli powder, lemon juice and the salt, and rub over each piece of chicken. Set aside for 10–15 minutes.
Meanwhile, prepare the marinade by combining the yoghurt, ginger and garlic pastes, garam masala, tandoori masala and salt. Coat the chicken pieces with the marinade, cover and refrigerate for 5–6 hours.
Bring to room temperature before cooking. Braai (barbecue) or grill, turning and basting every few minutes until cooked through, but still juicy (about 15–20 minutes).
Serve with daal, such as tarka daal (p 59), roti or naan (p 105), and dahi pudina chutney (p 123), with mashed potatoes or fries, sautéed vegetables and a green salad. Garnish with onion rings and lemon wedges.

TIP
Prepare extra and freeze to prepare makhni murgi (p 40).

SEEKH KABAB
SEEKH KEBABS
MAKES 8 KEBABS

300 g lean lamb, minced
1 t (5 ml) minced root ginger
2 t (10 ml) minced garlic
1 small onion, finely chopped
2 T (30 ml) finely chopped fresh coriander
1 green chilli, seeded and finely chopped (optional)
2 t (10 ml) lemon juice
2 t (10 ml) tandoori masala (p 122)
1 t (5 ml) garam masala (p 122)
1 T (15 ml) cashew nut paste (p 123)
salt to taste
8 wooden or metal skewers
2 T (30 ml) oil
2 T (30 ml) chopped fresh mint

Pre-heat the grill to very hot or use a braai (barbecue) if available.
In a bowl mix the minced lamb with all the other ingredients except the oil and chopped mint. Divide this mixture into 8 equal portions. Wrap each portion around a skewer in the shape of a hotdog sausage. Brush each kebab with a little oil and braai or grill, turning frequently until done (about 15 minutes). Serve hot, garnished with chopped mint, with the main meal.
Alternatively, remove the meat from the skewers, cut the kebabs into bite-size pieces, and serve on toothpicks with yoghurt pudina chutney (p 123) on the side as a starter.

TIP
The kebabs can be prepared and cooked ahead of time. Cover with foil and place in a single layer in a warm oven until ready to serve.

VARIATIONS
Chicken or beef mince may be used instead of lamb.

BOTI KABAB
LAMB KEBABS
SERVES 6 AS A STARTER OR 3 AS A MAIN COURSE

400 g boneless lamb, cut into 2.5 cm cubes
2 T (30 ml) oil, for basting
marinade
¾ cup (180 ml) low-fat yoghurt
2 t (10 ml) ginger paste
2 t (10 ml) garlic paste
1½ t (7.5 ml) tandoori masala (p 122)

1 t (5 ml) garam masala (p 122)
1 t (5 ml) chilli powder or to taste
1 t (5 ml) raw mango powder or
   1 t (5 ml) lemon juice
meat tenderiser, used according to label instructions
salt to taste

First make the marinade by mixing together the marinade ingredients in a bowl. Add the lamb and mix well. Cover and marinate in the refrigerator for 5–6 hours, or preferably overnight. Bring to room temperature before cooking. Thread the lamb pieces onto skewers. Braai (barbecue) or grill, turning and basting every few minutes until cooked through but still juicy (about 15–20 minutes).

Remove from skewers and serve on toothpicks with pudina chutney (p 123) as a starter, or as a main meal along with a legume dish, a vegetable dish, naan (p 105) or chapati (p 98), and raita.

VARIATIONS
Pork or veal are excellent substitutes for lamb.

TANDOORI LAMB CHOPS
SERVES 6

12 medium lean lamb chops
2 T (30 ml) oil, for basting
marinade
¾ cup (180 ml) low-fat yoghurt
1 T (15 ml) ginger paste
1 T (15 ml) garlic paste
1 T (15 ml) finely chopped mint leaves

2 t (10 ml) tandoori masala (p 122)
2 t (10 ml) garam masala (p 122)
1 T (15 ml) lemon juice
1 t (5 ml) chilli powder or to taste
meat tenderiser, used according to label instructions
salt to taste

First make the marinade by mixing together all the marinade ingredients in a bowl. Add the lamb chops and mix well. Cover and marinate in the refrigerator for 5–6 hours, or preferably overnight. Bring to room temperature before cooking. Braai (barbecue) or grill, turning and basting every few minutes until done (about 15–20 minutes).

Serve with a legume dish, a vegetable dish, naan (p 105) or chapati (p 98), and kachoomber raita (p 79).

BOTI KABAB **(TOP)** AND TANDOORI LAMB CHOPS **(BOTTOM)**

STUFFED BANGARA (GOAN STYLE)
STUFFED MACKEREL
SERVES 4

The west coast town of Goa with its sun-kissed beaches was ruled by the Portuguese for almost four centuries and today Goan food still retains its strong Portuguese influence. This dish and vindaloo (p 49) are among my favourites. Both are very spicy and pungent, so I have modified them to suit a western palate.

4 medium mackerel
1 T (15 ml) oil, for basting
lemon and tomato slices, for garnish
stuffing
5 large cloves garlic
1 x 1 cm-thick slice root ginger
1 T (15 ml) cumin seeds
1 T (15 ml) coriander seeds
1 t (5 ml) chilli powder, or to taste
6 whole peppercorns
3 T (45 ml) malt vinegar
2 T (30 ml) coconut cream powder
3 T (45 ml) finely chopped fresh coriander
1 t (5 ml) sugar
salt to taste

Clean and wash the mackerel and pat dry with paper kitchen towel. Cut along both sides of the bone (from the fin side) from head to tail, to open like a pocket for filling. Set aside.
Place all the stuffing ingredients in a blender and blend to a smooth paste. Fill the fish with a little paste on either side of the bone. Brush with a little oil and braai (barbecue) or grill, gently turning once until brown on both sides.
Garnish and serve as a starter or as a main dish with rice and a legume dish.

TIRANGA PANEER TIKKA

BARBECUED TRI-COLOUR CHEESE

MAKES 8 SKEWERS

1 t (5 ml) garam masala (p 122)
1 t (5 ml) ground cumin
1 t (5 ml) ground coriander
½ t (2.5 ml) fenugreek seeds, ground*
½ t (2.5 ml) chilli powder
½ t (2.5 ml) pepper
salt to taste
1 t (5 ml) ginger paste
1 t (5 ml) garlic paste
¼ cup (60 ml) yoghurt
1 T (15 ml) oil
1 T (15 ml) lemon juice
300 g paneer, cut into 3 cm cubes
1 large red pepper, seeded and cut into 3 cm squares
1 large green pepper, seeded and cut into 3 cm squares
8 long wooden skewers

In a large mixing bowl place all the ingredients, except for the paneer and peppers, and beat until the yoghurt is smooth and creamy. Add the paneer and peppers and mix gently until they are well coated.
Thread equally onto 8 skewers, alternating paneer and pepper pieces. Braai or cook under a hot grill, turning frequently until the peppers just start to brown.
As a starter, serve on toothpicks instead of skewers, along with pudina chutney (p 123) or with or without skewers with any daal, roti or rice and a little aloo raita (p 79) on the side for a perfectly balanced meal.

*Use a pestle and mortar to grind to a powder.

SOYA KABAB

SOYA CHUNK KEBABS

SERVES 4

1 cup (250 ml) dry soya chunks
8 wooden skewers
oil for basting
marinade
¼ cup (60 ml) yoghurt
2 T (30 ml) lemon juice
1 t (5 ml) ground cumin
½ t (2.5 ml) garam masala (p 122)
salt to taste
1 t (5 ml) tandoori masala (p 122)
½ t (2.5 ml) chilli powder
¼ t (1.25 ml) grated nutmeg
2 t (10 ml) garlic paste
1 t (5 ml) ginger paste

Prepare the soya chunks (see page 120) and set aside. Place all the marinade ingredients in a bowl and whip to mix thoroughly. Add the prepared soya chunks and mix to coat them well. Cover and marinate for 2–3 hours or more, turning the chunks over once.
Thread equally onto 8 skewers and braai or cook under a hot grill, turning frequently and basting with any leftover marinade and oil until the chunks are golden brown.
Serve on toothpicks instead of skewers as a starter, along with pudina chutney (p 123), or with or without skewers with any daal, chapati (p 98) or rice and a little palak raita (p 76) on the side.

Fish holds an important place in an Indian meal. Both sea fish and fresh-water fish are popular, and any firm white fish is suitable for the recipes in this chapter. I generally use kingklip, sole or hake, all with very satisfactory results. Good-quality fresh prawns, calamari and other fresh seafood are best for the recipes provided here. However, frozen cooked prawns and other frozen seafood may also be used with fairly satisfactory results. Thaw frozen seafood completely and pat dry before cooking.

North Indians tend to favour fried fish dishes, while those living along the coast prepare excellent dishes with rich gravies using coconut and coconut milk. As fresh coconut is not readily available in South Africa, I have substituted it with dried coconut cream powder in the recipes. Canned coconut milk and coconut cream are available at some supermarkets or at any oriental store.

Most of the recipes given here are from northern India, with a few from the south.

Note

Remember that the colour of dishes with gravy will largely depend on how well you brown the onion without burning it. Use non-stick pans to minimise the use of fat when sautéing or browning meat and onions, or keep sprinkling with a little water to prevent onion, ginger and garlic paste from sticking and burning. If you enjoy pungent food, replace the paprika with red chilli powder according to taste. Oil may also be used in place of unsalted butter without compromising the flavour.

FISH
AND SHELLFISH

TAMATER WALI MACHHI

FISH IN TOMATO GRAVY

SERVES 6

600 g firm white fish fillets
2 t (10 ml) ginger paste
1 t (5 ml) garlic paste
1 t (5 ml) lemon juice
1 t (5 ml) salt
½ t (2.5 ml) chilli powder or paprika
1 T (15 ml) coconut cream powder
¾ cup (180 ml) water
1 T (15 ml) coarsely chopped cashew nuts
2 t (10 ml) sunflower seeds
2 T (30 ml) oil
1 T (15 ml) finely chopped garlic
½ t (2.5 ml) turmeric
1 t (5 ml) ground cumin
1 t (5 ml) paprika
1 T (15 ml) tomato purée
2 large, ripe tomatoes, puréed
1½ t (7.5 ml) garam masala (p 122)
¼ cup (60 ml) finely chopped fresh coriander
salt to taste
¼ cup (60 ml) cream

Cut the fish fillets into small pieces (about 4 cm each). Place in a mixing bowl and add the ginger and garlic pastes, lemon juice, salt and chilli powder or paprika. Mix thoroughly and leave to marinate for about 30–40 minutes.

Soak the coconut cream powder in water for 5 minutes. Place cashew nuts, sunflower seeds and soaked coconut in a blender and blend until a smooth paste is formed. Set aside.

Heat the oil in a pan over medium heat. Add the garlic and sauté for a few seconds without letting it turn brown. Add the turmeric, cumin, chilli powder or paprika and tomato purée. Stir-fry for another 30–40 seconds. Stir in the coconut paste and continue stir-frying for 2–3 minutes longer. Add the fish, stir and cook gently until the fish is well coated with sauce. Stir in the puréed tomatoes, garam masala, half of the chopped coriander and salt to taste. When it starts to bubble, reduce the heat to low, cover and cook for about 10 minutes or until the fish flakes easily with a fork. With a slotted spoon remove the fish pieces to a serving dish and keep warm.

Add the cream to the remaining sauce in the pan. Stir and cook until the sauce starts to bubble again. Remove from heat and pour it over the fish. Garnish with the other half of the chopped coriander.

Serve with plain boiled rice, kachoomber raita (p 79) or any other salad of your choice. The fish can also be served with plain Italian bread instead of rice.

DAHI WALI MACHHI

FISH IN YOGHURT SAUCE

SERVES 6

600 g fish fillets (any firm white fish)
2 t (10 ml) garlic paste
1 t (5 ml) ginger paste
3 T (45 ml) lemon juice
1 t (5 ml) salt
1 T (15 ml) coriander seeds
1 T (15 ml) cumin seeds
6–8 large cloves garlic
1 x 2 cm piece root ginger
1 small green chilli, seeded and chopped (optional)
½ cup (125 ml) chopped fresh coriander

1 tomato, coarsely chopped
2 T (30 ml) oil
1 large onion, minced
½ t (2.5 ml) chilli powder, or to taste
1 t (5 ml) mustard powder
½ t (2.5 ml) turmeric
1½ t (7.5 ml) garam masala (p 122)
salt to taste
1 cup (250 ml) low-fat yoghurt, whisked
1 T (15 ml) chopped fresh coriander, for garnish

Wash and cut the fish into 4 cm pieces and pat dry. Place in a mixing bowl with garlic and ginger pastes, lemon juice and salt. Mix well and set aside for a few minutes.
In the meanwhile heat a small, shallow pan over medium heat, without oil, and roast the coriander and cumin seeds until brown, without burning. Remove from heat and allow to cool.
Place the garlic cloves, ginger, green chilli (if using), chopped coriander, tomato and roasted seeds in a blender and blend until a smooth paste is formed (use a little water if it is too dry). Set aside.
In a non-stick pan, heat the oil over medium heat. Add the onion and stir-fry until golden brown. Stir in the blended paste, all the dry spices and salt. Stir-fry for 1 minute longer. Add the fish and continue stir-frying for another 4–5 minutes or until the fish is nicely coated and has changed colour. Reduce the heat to as low as possible. Stir in the yoghurt and continue stirring gently until the sauce starts bubbling. Cover and cook over low heat for about 10 minutes or until the fish flakes easily with a fork. Garnish with chopped coriander.
Serve with plain boiled rice, kachoomber raita (p 79), or any other salad, and bread.

NARIAL WALI MACHHI

COCONUT FISH

SERVES 6

600 g fish fillets (any firm white fish)
3 T (45 ml) lemon juice
1 t (5 ml) salt
2 T (30 ml) coconut cream powder
½ cup (125 ml) tinned coconut milk
½ cup (125 ml) water
4 t (20 ml) coriander seeds
2 t (10 ml) cumin seeds
4–5 large cloves garlic
1 x 2 cm piece root ginger
1 green chilli (optional)
1 t (5 ml) sugar
2 T (30 ml) oil
1 large onion, finely chopped
1 large tomato, grated
1 t (5 ml) paprika
½ t (2.5 ml) turmeric
1 t (5 ml) ground cumin
1 T (15 ml) malt vinegar
salt to taste
2 t (10 ml) chopped fresh coriander, for garnish

Rub the fish with lemon juice and 1 t (5 ml) salt
and set aside. Place the coconut cream powder,
milk and water in a blender and let it soak for
5 minutes. Add the coriander and cumin seeds,
garlic, ginger, green chilli (if using) and sugar.
Blend to a smooth mixture. Set aside.
Heat oil in a non-stick pan over medium heat and
sauté the onion until golden brown. Stir in the
tomato, dry spices and vinegar. Stir-fry
for 3 minutes. Add coconut mixture and bring to a
boil. Reduce the heat to very low and add the fish.
Cover and cook for about 10 minutes or until the
fish flakes easily with a fork, lightly stirring in
between. Add salt, if necessary. Garnish with
chopped coriander.
Serve hot with plain cooked rice and a salad or
raita of your choice.

BALTI MASALA JHINGA

SPICY STIR-FRIED SHRIMPS

SERVES 6

2 T (30 ml) oil
1 T (30 ml) unsalted butter
2 medium onions, sliced
5 cloves garlic, finely chopped
2 T (30 ml) tomato purée
2 t (10 ml) cumin seeds, pounded
2 t (10 ml) coriander seeds, pounded
1 green chilli, seeded and finely chopped (optional)
1 t (5 ml) garam masala (p 122)
½ red pepper, seeded and cut into thin strips
½ green pepper, seeded and cut into thin strips
700 g shrimps, shelled and de-veined
salt to taste

Heat the oil and butter in a frying pan or wok over
medium heat. Add the onions and garlic and sauté
until translucent. Add the tomato purée and all
spices and stir-fry for 1–2 minutes.

Stir in the peppers and sauté for a minute longer.
Add the shrimps and stir-fry for 4–5 minutes or until
the shrimps have turned pink and are cooked
through. Do not overcook. Add salt to taste and
remove from heat.

Serve as a starter or as a main course with
a legume dish, a side dish of vegetables and
paratha (p 101).

SAMUNDRI KHAZANA

SEAFOOD IN ALMOND SAUCE

SERVES 6

2 T (30 ml) oil
1 T (15 ml) unsalted butter
2 large onions, minced
1 T (15 ml) garlic paste
2 t (10 ml) ginger paste
3 T (45 ml) tomato purée
2 large tomatoes, grated
¼ cup (60 ml) almond paste (p 123)
¼ t (1.25 ml) ground mace
2 t (10 ml) ground cumin
1 t (5 ml) turmeric
½ t (2.5 ml) chilli powder, or to taste
1 t (5 ml) paprika
1 t (5 ml) garam masala (p 122)
salt to taste
200 g shrimps, shelled and de-veined
200 g calamari rings
200 g fish fillets, cut into small cubes
3 cups (750 ml) hot water
2 T (30 ml) finely chopped fresh coriander

Heat the oil and butter in a non-stick pan over medium heat. Add the onions and sauté until golden brown. Stir in the garlic and ginger pastes and stir-fry for 30 seconds. Add the tomato purée, grated tomatoes and almond paste. Continue stir-frying for 1 minute longer.

Stir in all the spices, salt and all seafood. Stir-fry for another 2–3 minutes. Add the water and half of the chopped coriander. Bring to a boil. Cover, reduce heat and simmer for 5–7 minutes or until the fish flakes easily with a fork. Remove from heat and transfer to a serving bowl. Sprinkle over the remaining coriander and serve hot.

Serve with gobi aloo (p 68), onion rings dressed with lemon juice, salt and pepper to taste, and chapati (p 98) or rice.

TIP

This recipe freezes very well.

CHICKEN
AND LAMB

Non-vegetarian Indians like to have at least one meal a day that includes a fish, chicken or meat dish.

A few years ago, chicken was fairly expensive in India and was usually prepared only for special

guests. Fortunately this has changed now, owing to the mass production of chickens in India. Apart from

tandoori dishes, there are so many other wonderful ways of cooking chicken and I had a hard task

shortlisting recipes to include in this section. In the end I decided to provide simplified recipes that are

easy to prepare, yet delicious to eat. Remember to pick smaller birds for more succulent results.

For religious reasons Hindus exclude beef, while pork is forbidden for Muslims. Goat meat – known

as mutton – is very often the red meat of choice, and it is commonly available. Lamb or sheep are

also commonly used.

Meat is generally cut into small pieces and cooked with the bone in. The recipes in this section mostly

call for boneless meat, chops or minced meat.

In northern India, meat is cooked with vegetables such as potatoes (a great favourite), spinach, turnips

or green peas.

MAKHNI MURGI

TANDOORI CHICKEN IN BUTTER SAUCE

SERVES 4

1 recipe tandoori murgi (p 25)
2 T (30 ml) unsalted butter
2 T (30 ml) garlic paste
1 T (15 ml) ginger paste
4 T (60 ml) tomato purée, mixed with
½ cup (125 ml) water
½ t (2.5 ml) fenugreek seeds, ground*
1 t (5 ml) garam masala (p 122)
1 t (5 ml) paprika
½ t (2.5 ml) ground black pepper
½ t (2.5 ml) white sugar
salt to taste
2 t (10 ml) finely chopped fresh coriander
½ cup (125 ml) cream, mixed with
1 cup (250 ml) water
1 T (15 ml) chopped fresh coriander, for garnish

Prepare the Tandoori murgi chicken and keep it warm. Heat butter in a large, non-stick frying pan over medium heat. Stir in garlic and ginger pastes and sauté for a few seconds. Stir in all the rest of the ingredients except for the cream and water, and coriander. Stir and cook for 1 minute and then stir in the cream mixture.

Bring to a simmer, add the cooked chicken and cook while stirring gently for 2 minutes or until heated through. Transfer to a serving dish and garnish with the chopped fresh coriander. Serve hot with naan (p 105) or chapati (p 98), a vegetable side dish and kachoomber raita (p 79).

*Gives a very subtle flavour to this dish. Omit if you do not have it in stock.

MURGI KA KORMA

CHICKEN IN FRIED ONION AND YOGHURT SAUCE

SERVES 4

oil for frying
2 onions, thinly sliced
1 cup (250 ml) low-fat yoghurt
¼ cup (60 ml) ricotta cheese
2 T (30 ml) slivered almonds
2 onions, minced
2 t (10 ml) garlic paste
2 bay leaves
6 cardamom pods, cracked
1 x 3 cm piece stick cinnamon
1 t (5 ml) ground cumin
pinch grated nutmeg
½ t (2.5 ml) pepper
½ t (2.5 ml) chilli powder or 1 t (5 ml) paprika
½ t (2.5 ml) garam masala (p 122)
salt to taste
8 skinless chicken legs, thighs or breasts
2 cups (500 ml) hot water

Heat sufficient oil in a round-bottomed pan or wok over medium heat. Fry the sliced onions until golden brown and crisp. Spread over paper towel to drain off the excess oil. Place the yoghurt, ricotta cheese, almonds and fried onions (saving a few for garnish) in a blender and blend to a smooth paste (use a little water if it is too dry). Set aside.

In a large, non-stick pan, heat 2 T (30 ml) oil (use the same oil in which the onions were fried), over medium heat. Add minced onions and sauté until golden brown. Stir in the garlic paste, all spices, garam masala and salt. Add the chicken. Stir and cook for 5 minutes. Stir in the prepared yoghurt almond paste and continue stir-frying for another 10 minutes. Add the water and mix well. Reduce heat, cover and simmer, stirring to prevent sticking, for another 10–15 minutes or until the chicken is tender. Serve garnished with the saved fried onions. The whole spices may be removed before serving.

Serve with naan (p 105), chapati or paratha (pp 98–102), patta gobi aur mattar (p 68) and raita.

MURGI KA KORMA

MAKHNI MURGI

BALTI MURGI SOA WALI

STIR-FRIED CHICKEN WITH DILL

SERVES 4

8 skinless chicken thighs
1 T (15 ml) oil
1 T (15 ml) butter
1½ cups (375 ml) water
1 medium onion, coarsely chopped
3 large cloves garlic, finely chopped
2 t (10 ml) finely chopped root ginger
1 green chilli, seeded and finely chopped (optional)
1 t (5 ml) paprika
1 t (5 ml) ground cumin
1 t (5 ml) garam masala (p 122)
salt to taste
¼ cup (60 ml) finely chopped fresh dill
1 large tomato, seeded and coarsely chopped

Trim any visible fat from the chicken. Wash and pat dry with paper towel. Set aside.
Heat the oil and butter in a non-stick pan over medium heat. Add the chicken thighs and fry, turning once, for 5–7 minutes, or until lightly browned on both sides. Add the water and bring to a boil. Reduce heat, cover and simmer, stirring to prevent sticking, for 10–15 minutes or until the chicken is tender. Increase the heat to medium and stir-fry until all the liquid has evaporated.
Using a slotted spoon, remove the chicken to a plate and return the pan to the stove over medium heat. Add the onion, garlic, ginger and green chilli, if using, and stir-fry for about 2 minutes or until the onion is translucent. Stir in the spices, garam masala, salt and dill and continue to stir-fry for a minute longer. Reduce heat, add tomato and chicken and cook over low heat for 3–4 minutes or until the chicken is heated through.
Serve with any daal dish, raita, roti or rice.

BALTI RANGEELA MURGI

COLOURFUL STIR-FRIED CHICKEN

SERVES 6

400 g skinless chicken breast fillets
2 T (30 ml) oil
1 t (5 ml) cumin seeds
1 onion, coarsely chopped
1 T (15 ml) finely chopped garlic
salt to taste
1 t (5 ml) garam masala (p 122)
½ t (2.5 ml) pepper
½ t (2.5 ml) paprika
1 t (5 ml) ground cumin
1 green chilli, seeded and finely chopped (optional)
1 cup (250 ml) coarsely sliced mushrooms
4 baby corn cobs, sliced
2 medium baby marrows, sliced
4 baby carrots, sliced
½ red pepper, seeded and diced into 2 cm squares
½ green pepper, seeded and diced into 2 cm squares

Cut the chicken into 2 cm cubes and set aside.
Heat the oil in a wok or a large non-stick pan over medium heat. Add the cumin seeds and fry for 30 seconds or until the cumin starts to crackle. Add the chicken and stir-fry for 4–5 minutes. Stir in the onion, garlic and salt and continue stir-frying for 3 minutes longer. Add all the remaining ingredients except for the peppers. Lower heat and continue to cook, stirring, for 5–7 minutes longer or until the vegetables are almost tender. Stir in the peppers and cook for another 3 minutes. If too moist, increase heat to medium when you add the peppers and cook until the chicken is done and the vegetables are tender but crunchy.
As the name suggests, this is a very colourful dish. Serve with tarka daal (p 59), angoor aur akhrot raita (p 75), roti, naan (p 105) or rice.

SHAHI KOFTA
ROYAL MEATBALLS IN GRAVY
SERVES 6 (MAKES 12 KOFTAS)

meatballs
6 dried apricots, finely chopped
2 T (30 ml) finely chopped mint leaves
2 T (30 ml) chopped almonds
3 T (45 ml) ricotta cheese
pinch of salt
500 g minced lamb
1 t (5 ml) ginger paste
½ t (2.5 ml) garam masala (p 122)
½ t (2.5 ml) chilli powder or paprika
½ t (2.5 ml) salt or to taste

gravy
3 T (45 ml) oil
2 onions, minced
2 bay leaves
1 cardamom pod, cracked
1 t (5 ml) garlic paste
1 t (5 ml) ginger paste
½ t (2.5 ml) turmeric
1 t (5 ml) paprika
1 t (5 ml) garam masala
salt to taste
2 ripe tomatoes, grated
2 T (30 ml) chopped fresh coriander
4–5 cups (1–1.25 litres) hot water

To make the meatballs, place the apricots, mint leaves, almonds, cheese and a pinch of salt in a bowl and mix well. In a separate bowl, mix together the remaining ingredients for the meatballs and divide into 12 equal portions. Grease your palm lightly and flatten one portion slightly. Place a teaspoon of apricot mixture in the centre and fold the edges inwards to form a small ball (kofta). Set aside. Repeat the process until all the meatball mixture is used up.

To make the gravy, heat the oil in a wide-based, non-stick skillet over medium heat. Add the minced onions, bay leaves and cardamom and stir-fry until golden brown. Stir in all the remaining gravy ingredients except for the tomatoes, coriander and water. Continue frying until the oil just starts to float. Add the tomatoes, 1 T (15 ml) of coriander and 2 cups (500 ml) of hot water and bring to a boil.

Reduce heat to low and carefully place the meatballs in the skillet, in a single layer. Cover and continue cooking over low heat for 8–10 minutes. Shake the pan back and forth every minute or two to avoid sticking and to cook the meatballs evenly.

When all the water has evaporated, continue stir-frying gently for 5 minutes longer. Add the remaining water, increase the heat and bring to a boil. Reduce heat, cover and simmer for 5 minutes more. Transfer to a serving dish and garnish with the remaining coriander.

Serve hot with gobi aloo (p 68), kachoomber raita (p 79) and chapati (p 98) or rice or over cooked pasta with your favourite side salad.

VARIATION
Minced beef or chicken can be used instead of lamb.

KHEEMA MATTER

LAMB MINCE WITH GREEN PEAS

SERVES 6

3 T (45 ml) oil
2 large onions, minced in the blender
4 t (20 ml) garlic paste
2 t (10 ml) ginger paste
1 green chilli, seeded and finely chopped
2 T (30 ml) tomato purée
2 T (30 ml) chopped fresh coriander
1 t (5 ml) ground fenugreek (optional)
1 t (5 ml) turmeric
½ t (2.5 ml) chilli powder
½ t (2.5 ml) paprika
1 t (5 ml) ground cumin
1 t (5 ml) ground coriander
1 t (5 ml) garam masala (p 122)
salt to taste
400 g minced lamb or beef
2 large tomatoes, finely chopped
2 cups (500 ml) hot water
2 cups (500 ml) frozen green peas
1 t (5ml) chopped fresh coriander, for garnish

Heat the oil in a non-stick skillet over medium heat. Add the minced onions, and stir-fry until golden brown. Stir in all the remaining ingredients except for the last five. Continue to stir-fry until the oil just starts to float. Add the mince, chopped tomatoes and hot water. Stir well, cover and simmer for about 10 minutes, stirring now and then. Add the peas, reduce heat and cook for another 10 minutes or until the mince is cooked and water has evaporated. Remove the lid and stir and cook for 5 minutes longer. Transfer to a serving dish and garnish with the remaining chopped coriander.
Serve with hot paratha (pp 101–102), sabat moong masaledar (p 61) and onion rings dressed with lemon juice, salt and pepper to taste.

KHEEMA MATTER

PALAK GOSHT

LAMB WITH SPINACH

SERVES 6

2 onions, coarsely chopped
6–7 cloves garlic, chopped
1 x 3 cm piece root ginger, chopped
1 green chilli, chopped (optional)
500 g fresh or frozen spinach, chopped
few sprigs fresh dill, chopped
2 tomatoes, chopped
2 T (30 ml) oil
1 T (15 ml) unsalted butter
500 g boneless lamb
2 x 2 cm pieces stick cinnamon
½ t (2.5 ml) turmeric
2 t (10 ml) garam masala (p 122)
½ t (2.5 ml) chilli powder
salt to taste
1½–2 cups (375–500 ml) water, in batches as required

In a blender, first blend the onions, garlic, ginger and green chilli (if using) to a purée and remove. Then blend together the spinach and dill, and remove. Finally, blend the tomatoes to a purée and set aside.
Heat the oil and butter in a non-stick pan over medium heat. Add the lamb and cinnamon and stir-fry for about 5 minutes. Add the onion mixture and continue to stir-fry until the lamb and onion mixture is golden brown. Add the puréed tomatoes, all spices and salt. Stir and cook for another 5 minutes. Stir in the spinach, cover, reduce heat and simmer for 15–20 minutes or until the lamb is tender, stirring to prevent sticking. Add a little water if required. Palak gosht sauce should be like a thick purée.
Serve with rasedar lobia, kheera pudina raita (p 75) and chapati (p 98) or naan (p 105).

VARIATIONS

Veal, beef or chicken may be used instead of lamb.

TIP

To reduce cooking time, I sometimes use meat tenderiser. (See label instructions for the amount.)

SHAHI KORMA

LAMB IN ALMOND AND YOGHURT SAUCE

SERVES 4

Korma dishes are generally mild, with a creamy gravy.
Vegetables can be used instead of meat (see Variation below).

¼ cup (60 ml) low-fat yoghurt
¼ t (1.25 ml) cardamom seeds, pounded
1 x 2.5 cm piece root ginger
1 T (15 ml) chopped garlic
3 T (45 ml) almonds, blanched and chopped
2 T (30 ml) oil
500 g boneless lamb, cut into 2 cm cubes
2 onions, finely chopped

2 bay leaves
4 whole cloves
½ t (2.5 ml) paprika
1½ t (7.5 ml) ground cumin
salt to taste
½ cup (125 ml) cream, mixed with
1¼ cup (310 ml) water
½ t (2.5 ml) garam masala (p 122)

Place the yoghurt, cardamom, ginger, garlic and almonds in a blender and blend to a smooth paste. Set aside.
In a wide-based, non-stick pan heat the oil over medium heat. Add the lamb, onions, bay leaves and cloves and stir-fry for 10 minutes or until the lamb and onions have browned. Stir in the almond yoghurt paste and the paprika, ground cumin and salt. Continue to stir and cook until all the liquid has evaporated. Stir-fry for another minute. Stir in the cream and water mixture. When it starts to boil, reduce the heat to low, cover and simmer for 35–40 minutes longer, stirring to prevent sticking, or until the lamb is tender and you have a thick brown gravy. Add more liquid if too dry. Remove from heat.

Serve hot, sprinkled with ½ t (2.5 ml) of garam masala. Include chapati (p 98), naan (p 105) or rice and kachoomber raita (p 79) in the menu.
This dish is also well complemented by mashed potatoes, steamed vegetables and a side salad.

VARIATION

For a vegetarian korma, replace the meat with about 700 g mixed vegetables, such as cauliflower, potatoes, beans and carrots. Follow the same method of cooking.

SHAHI KORMA

VINDALOO

HOT AND SOUR LAMB

SERVES 6

**The amount of chilli powder used can be varied according to taste. In Goa, vindaloo is made very hot.
The amount of chilli powder and peppercorns used in this recipe makes the dish mild in my book!**

1 T (15 ml) cumin seeds
¼ t (1.25 ml) cardamom seeds
2 x 2 cm pieces stick cinnamon
8 whole cloves
10 whole peppercorns
1 cup (250 ml) vinegar, preferably malt vinegar
1 t (5 ml) mustard powder
1 t (5 ml) chilli powder, or to taste
1 t (5 ml) paprika
1 t (5 ml) turmeric
1 t (5 ml) white sugar
800 g boneless lamb, cut into 5 cm cubes
3 T (45 ml) oil
1 onion, finely chopped
2 t (10 ml) ginger paste
1 T (15 ml) garlic paste
salt to taste
3 cups (750 ml) hot water

Grind the cumin seeds, cardamom seeds, cinnamon, cloves and peppercorns in a coffee grinder. Transfer to a bowl. Add the vinegar to the ground spices. Stir in the mustard, chilli powder, paprika, turmeric and sugar, and mix well. Add the lamb and mix thoroughly. Leave to marinate for 5–6 hours, or preferably overnight.

Heat the oil in a non-stick pan over medium heat. Add the onion and sauté until golden brown. Stir in the ginger and garlic pastes and stir-fry for 30 seconds. Stir in the marinated lamb and salt and stir and cook for 2–3 minutes Add the water and bring to a boil. Reduce heat to low, cover and simmer for an hour or so, stirring now and then, or until the lamb is tender.

Best served with plain rice. My family enjoys it with crusty Italian bread as well.

VARIATIONS
Beef or chicken can be used instead of lamb.
This dish can also be cooked in the oven. Follow the above instructions up until after the water is added. Pre-heat the oven to 180 °C and cook vindaloo covered for 1–1½ hours or until the lamb is tender.

VEGETARIAN
DISHES

This section includes various delicious ways of cooking paneer (home-made cheese) and legumes (dried peas and beans, and pulses, including lentils).

Cooked pulses ('daal' in Hindi, of which there are many kinds in India) generally form the nucleus of a menu plan for vegetarians, as they are a good source of protein, some B vitamins and fibre. Proteins from this source have one or more essential amino acids missing when eaten individually, and are therefore termed incomplete proteins and are considered lesser proteins than animal proteins. Soya is the only exception, being equal in quality to animal protein. However, eaten in combination with certain other foods, legumes will meet the total protein requirement of vegetarians very effectively. Since the body does not store amino acids as it does carbohydrates and fat, it is advisable – especially for growing children and vegetarians – to include these combinations in the same meal to ensure the availability of all the essential amino acids. Legumes should be combined with any of the following:

  grains

  nuts and seeds

  milk products.

A typical Indian meal is an excellent example of the correct combination for a nutritionally completely balanced meal, which is why Indian food provides such an attractive option for vegetarians. Rice or wheat roti (grains) are combined with a legume preparation and yoghurt, buttermilk or other milk product at each meal, along with a vegetable preparation.

A great variety of legumes is grown in India and there are many different ways of cooking them, both with meat and vegetables. The recipes that follow provide interesting ways of adding variety to your daily food plan. To make things simpler, I have provided recipes using only those legumes that I have seen on supermarket shelves. For convenience I have used canned legumes in place of the dried variety, as this saves so much soaking and cooking time.

Cooking times of the dry product vary according to the type of pulse or lentil used, and whole beans and pulses take longer to cook than the split variety. I generally use a pressure cooker to cut down on cooking time. I also soak green moong beans in warm water for 2–3 hours, or preferably overnight. As a general rule, any cooked daal (pulse) should not be too watery, but should have a fairly mushy consistency. For tempering or seasoning we use ghee (clarified butter), which is not available in South Africa unless you go to an Indian store. I have used half oil and half butter in some recipes. Feel free to substitute oil for butter.

Most of the dishes can be frozen for several weeks.

MATTAR PANEER
HOME-MADE CHEESE WITH GREEN PEAS
SERVES 6

A very nutritious vegetarian dish.

350 g low-fat paneer (p 119)
3 T (45 ml) oil
2 onions, minced
1 t (5 ml) garlic paste
2 t (10 ml) ginger paste
1 t (5 ml) turmeric
2 t (10 ml) ground cumin
2 t (10 ml) ground coriander
1 t (5 ml) paprika
½ t (2.5 ml) chilli powder (optional)
1 t (5 ml) garam masala (p 122)
2 large tomatoes, grated
2 T (30 ml) finely chopped fresh coriander
2 cups (500 ml) green peas (frozen)
salt to taste
3 cups (750 ml) hot water
1 t (5 ml) chopped fresh coriander, for garnish

Cut the paneer into 2 cm cubes and set aside.
Heat the oil in a non-stick pan over medium heat.
Add the onions and stir-fry until golden brown. Stir
in the garlic and ginger pastes and fry for another
30 seconds. Add all the dry spices and tomatoes
and continue to stir-fry until some oil starts to
separate. Stir in 2 T (30 ml) fresh coriander, peas,
salt and paneer. Stir-fry for another minute and add
the water. Bring to the boil, cover and cook for
5 minutes or until the peas are tender and you have
a thick, aromatic sauce. Remove from heat and
transfer to a serving bowl. Sprinkle with 1 t (5 ml)
fresh coriander.
Serve hot with aloo soya tikki (p 17), pudina
chutney (p 123) and chapati (p 98), paratha
(pp 101–102) or rice.

BALTI PANEER
STIR-FRIED HOME-MADE CHEESE
SERVES 6

1 T (15 ml) coriander seeds
2 t (10 ml) cumin seeds
½ t (2.5 ml) whole peppercorns
½ t (2.5 ml) fenugreek seeds*
2 T (30 ml) oil
1 T (15 ml) unsalted butter
2 onions, finely chopped
2 t (10 ml) finely chopped garlic
1 t (5 ml) garam masala (p 122)
½ t (2.5 ml) chilli powder (optional)
½ t (2.5 ml) paprika
salt to taste
2 tomatoes, chopped
½ red pepper, cut into julienne strips
½ green pepper, cut into julienne strips
500 g low-fat paneer (p 119), cut into 2 cm cubes

Place coriander, cumin, peppercorns and fenugreek
seeds in a coffee grinder or blender and grind
coarsely by just pulsing the machine (on and off), or
use a mortar and pestle for the purpose. Set aside.
Heat oil and butter in a wok or any other round-
bottomed pan over medium heat. Add onions and
garlic and sauté until the onions just start to turn
golden. Add the pounded spices along with other
spices and salt. Stir-fry for 30 seconds, then stir in
the tomatoes and peppers. Continue to stir and cook
until the peppers are tender but still crunchy. Stir in
the paneer, lower the heat and stir-fry for about
5–7 minutes or until the paneer is heated through.
Remove from heat.
Serve with masoor daal sabzi wali (p 59),
kachoomber raita (p 79), paratha (pp 101–102)
and onion rings dressed with lemon juice and salt
and pepper to taste.

* Though important for the right flavour, omit if not
available.

MATTAR PANEER

BALTI PANEER

SOYA MATTAR

SOYA WITH GREEN PEAS

SERVES 6

1½ cups (375 ml) dry soya granules
1 T (15 ml) cumin seeds
1 T (15 ml) coriander seeds
6 whole cloves
¼ t (1.25 ml) cardamom seeds
1 x 2 cm piece stick cinnamon, broken into small bits
½ t (2.5 ml) fennel seeds
2 T (30 ml) oil
1 T (15 ml) unsalted butter
2 large onions, minced
4 t (20 ml) garlic paste

2 t (10 ml) finely chopped root ginger
1 green chilli, seeded and chopped (optional)
½ t (2.5 ml) turmeric
1 t (5 ml) paprika
salt to taste
3 T (45 ml) tomato purée
2 tomatoes, grated
1 t (5 ml) garam masala (p 122)
2 cups (500 ml) hot water
3 cups (750 ml) green peas
2 T (30 ml) finely chopped fresh coriander

Prepare soya granules (see page 120). Set aside. Lightly roast all the whole spices in a frying pan over low heat, without adding any oil, until brown and aromatic. Cool and grind to a powder in a coffee grinder. Set aside.

Heat the oil and butter in a non-stick pan over medium heat. Add the onions and sauté until light golden in colour. Stir in the garlic, ginger and green chilli if using. Sauté for a minute longer.

Stir in the roasted spices, other dry spices, salt, tomato purée, grated tomatoes and garam masala and stir and cook for 5 minutes or until oil starts to surface. Add the prepared soya and stir-fry for 3–4 minutes. Add the water, stir and bring to a boil. Reduce heat and cook covered, stirring now and then, for 10–15 minutes or until little liquid remains. Add the peas and cook for another 5–7 minutes or until the peas are cooked and no liquid remains. Add the coriander and stir and cook for another 5 minutes. Remove from heat.

Since this is a dry dish, serve it with sabat moong masaledar (p 61) or sabat masoor (p 65), angoor aur akhrot raita (p 75), chapati (p 98), naan (p 105) or rice.

SOYA KORMA

SOYA WITH CREAMY GRAVY

SERVES 6

Soya korma is rich in protein, calcium, vitamins and fibre and should be included in your meal plan often, especially if you are a vegetarian.

¾ cup (180 ml) dry soya granules
1 T (15 ml) poppy seeds
2 t (10 ml) sesame seeds
6 cloves garlic
2 t (10 ml) chopped fresh root ginger
¾ cup (180 ml) low-fat or home-made yoghurt
2 t (10 ml) garam masala (p 122)
1 t (5 ml) ground coriander
2 t (10 ml) ground cumin
½ t (2.5 ml) chilli powder, or to taste
½ t (2.5 ml) paprika
½ t (2.5 ml) pepper
salt to taste
2 T (30 ml) oil

1 T (15 ml) unsalted butter
3 cardamom pods, cracked
2 bay leaves
1 x 3 cm piece stick cinnamon
2 onions, finely chopped or grated
8 baby potatoes, peeled
1½ cups (375 ml) hot water (or more if needed)
1 cup (250 ml) frozen green peas
¼ cup (60 ml) tomato purée
1 T (15 ml) lemon juice
¼ cup (60 ml) cream
2 t (10 ml) finely chopped fresh coriander
1 t (5 ml) finely chopped mint leaves, for garnish

Prepare soya granules (see page 120). Set aside. Dry-roast the poppy and sesame seeds in a small frying pan over low heat until light golden in colour. Allow to cool for a minute or so. Place the roasted seeds in a blender along with the garlic and ginger and blend until a smooth paste is formed. If it is too dry to blend, add a little water. Transfer to a small bowl and set aside.

Combine the yoghurt and all the dry spices and salt in a bowl and whisk until smooth. Place the oil and butter in a wide-based non-stick pan and heat over medium heat. Add cardamom, bay leaves and cinnamon and fry for 30 seconds. Stir in the onions and sauté until golden brown. Add the seed paste

and stir-fry for 30–40 seconds. Add the prepared soya granules and stir and cook for another minute. Stir in the yoghurt mixture, potatoes and water and bring to a boil, stirring continuously. Reduce heat to low, cover and cook, stirring now and then, for 12–15 minutes or until the potatoes are cooked.

Stir in all the remaining ingredients except for the mint. If it is too dry, add some more hot water to get the required consistency. Stir and cook for 2–3 minutes longer or until the korma (gravy) starts to simmer again. Remove from heat. Transfer to a serving dish and garnish with chopped mint.

Serve hot with any side vegetable dish and yoghurt dish, with chapati (p 98) or bread rolls.

MASOOR DAAL SABZI WALI

TARKA DAAL
SEASONED LENTILS

SERVES 4–5

2½ cups (625 ml) water (or more if required)
1 t (5 ml) salt, or to taste
1 cup (250 ml) red lentils, picked over and washed
1 small clove garlic, chopped and crushed
½ t (2.5 ml) turmeric

seasoning
1 T (15 ml) oil
1 T (15 ml) butter
1 small onion, finely chopped
1 t (5 ml) cumin seeds
1 green chilli, seeded and chopped (optional)
1 T (15 ml) finely chopped fresh coriander
½ t (2.5 ml) paprika
2 medium tomatoes, finely chopped

In a pan bring the water to a boil over medium heat. Add the salt, lentils, garlic and turmeric, stir and bring to a boil again. Reduce heat, cover partially and cook for 25–30 minutes, stirring now and then, or until the lentils are soft and mushy. Remove from heat and prepare seasoning. Heat the oil and butter in a small frying pan over medium heat. Add the onion, cumin seeds and green chilli if using, and sauté for 5 minutes or until the onion turns golden brown. Stir in all the remaining ingredients and stir and cook for 4–5 minutes longer or until the tomatoes are soft. Remove from heat and add to the cooked lentils. Stir and cover tightly. Stand for 5 minutes before serving to allow the flavours to merge.
Serve with plain rice or biryani, vegetable pulao or roti and any vegetable or meat dish.

TIP

Can be prepared in advance and reheated just before serving.

MASOOR DAAL SABZI WALI

RED LENTILS WITH VEGETABLES

SERVES 6

4 cups (1 litre) water
1 cup (250 ml) red lentils, picked over and washed
1 t (5 ml) garlic paste
1 t (5 ml) turmeric
salt to taste
1 cup (250 ml) thinly sliced carrots
1 cup (250 ml) sliced baby marrows
1 cup (250 ml) broccoli florets
1 medium potato, peeled and cut into 2 cm cubes

seasoning
1 T (15 ml) oil
1 T (15 ml) butter
1 medium onion, finely chopped
2 t (10 ml) ground cumin
2 t (10 ml) ground coriander
½ t (2.5 ml) chilli powder
½ t (2.5 ml) paprika
2 tomatoes, chopped
1 T (15 ml) finely chopped fresh coriander

In a pan bring the water to a boil over medium heat. Add lentils, garlic, turmeric and salt. Reduce heat, cover partially and simmer for 15–20 minutes, or until the lentils are almost cooked. Stir in all the vegetables, cover and continue cooking for another 10–15 minutes or until the vegetables are tender but still crunchy. Remove from heat and keep warm.
Heat the oil and butter in a small frying pan over medium heat. Add the onion and sauté until golden brown. Add all the dry spices and tomatoes. Stir-fry for about 3–5 minutes or until the tomatoes are soft. Stir in the chopped coriander. Remove from heat and add to cooked lentils and vegetables. Stir and cover tightly. Stand for 5 minutes before serving to allow the flavours to merge.
Serve with plain rice or roti and any meat dish and yoghurt side dish for a perfectly balanced meal or with any tandoori preparation, with naan (p 105).

SABAT MOONG MASALEDAR

SPICY GREEN MOONG BEANS

SERVES 6

1½ cups (375 ml) green moong beans, picked over
and soaked overnight in water to cover
7 cups (1.75 litres) water (or more if required)
1 t (5 ml) ginger paste
2 t (10 ml) garlic paste
½ t (2.5 ml) turmeric
½ t (2.5 ml) chilli powder
salt to taste
seasoning
1 T (15 ml) oil
1 T (15 ml) unsalted butter
1 onion, finely chopped
½ green chilli, seeded and chopped
2 t (10 ml) ground cumin
2 t (10 ml) ground coriander
1 tomato, finely chopped

Drain and set aside the moong beans.

In a pan bring the water to a boil over medium heat. Add the moong, ginger and garlic pastes, turmeric, chilli powder and salt, stir and bring to a boil again. Reduce heat, cover partially and simmer for 45–60 minutes, stirring now and then, or until the moong are cooked and mushy.

While the moong is cooking, prepare the seasoning. Heat the oil and butter in a small frying pan over medium heat. Add the onion and sauté until golden brown. Add all the dry spices and tomato. Stir and cook for 3–5 minutes or until the tomato is soft and a little oil starts to float. Remove from heat and add to the cooked moong. Stir and cover tightly. Allow to stand for 5 minutes before serving to allow the flavours to merge.

Best served with any dry main dish or tandoori dish, a side vegetable of your choice and chapati (p 98) or plain rice.

VARIATION

The moong beans can be substituted with green or brown lentils.

SHAHI DAAL

ROYAL YELLOW SPLIT PEAS

SERVES 4

1 cup (250 ml) yellow split peas
4 cups (1 litre) water
salt to taste
½ t (2.5 ml) turmeric
½ t (2.5 ml) chilli powder
1 T (15 ml) unsalted butter
1 t (5 ml) garlic paste
¼ cup (60 ml) cream
1 cup (250 ml) low-fat yoghurt, whipped
seasoning
2 T (30 ml) unsalted butter
1 onion, finely chopped
2 t (10 ml) finely chopped garlic
½ t (2.5 ml) cumin seeds
1 t (5 ml) ground cumin
½ t (2.5 ml) white pepper
½ t (2.5 ml) paprika

Pick over and wash the split peas. Drain and set aside.
In a pan bring the water to a boil over medium heat.
Add the split peas, salt, turmeric, chilli powder,
butter and garlic paste. Stir and bring to a boil again.
Reduce heat, cover partially and simmer for
20–25 minutes, stirring now and then, or until
the split peas are cooked but not mushy.
Stir in the cream and then yoghurt, and continue to
stir and cook for another 10 minutes.
Remove from heat.
To make the seasoning, heat the butter in
a small frying pan over medium heat. Add the onion,
garlic and cumin seeds and sauté until the onion
is golden brown. Add the remaining ingredients,
remove from heat immediately and add to the
cooked split peas.
Makes an excellent meal when served with
gobi aloo (p 68), raita and chapati (p 98).

CHOLE AUR KHUMB

CHICKPEAS WITH MUSHROOMS

SERVES 6

1 x 400 g can chickpeas
200 g fresh button mushrooms
3 T (45 ml) oil
2 onions, minced or grated
1 T (15 ml) garlic paste
2 t (10 ml) ginger paste
3 T (45 ml) tomato purée
3 tomatoes, grated
½ t (2.5 ml) turmeric
½ t (2.5 ml) chilli powder
½ t (2.5 ml) paprika
2 t (10 ml) ground cumin
2 t (10 ml) garam masala (p 122)
salt to taste
2 cups (500 ml) hot water
2 t (10 ml) chopped fresh coriander, for garnish

Drain the chickpeas, then wash and drain again.
Set aside.
Wash and cut the mushrooms vertically in two or
four pieces depending on the size. Set aside.
Heat the oil in a non-stick pan over medium heat.
Stir in the onions and sauté until brown. Add the
garlic and ginger pastes and stir-fry for 30 seconds.
Add the tomato purée and grated tomatoes.
Continue to stir and cook for 5 minutes or until the
oil just starts to float. Stir in all the spices and salt
and stir well to mix. Add the mushrooms and sauté
for 5 minutes, stirring. Add the chickpeas and stir to
combine. Add the water and bring to a boil. Reduce
the heat and simmer covered for 5 minutes. Remove
from heat, transfer to a serving bowl and garnish
with coriander.
Serve with any vegetable side dish, a yoghurt
dish and chapati (p 98) or rice for a perfect
vegetable/protein combination, or with any
tandoori preparation.

SHAHI DAAL

CHOLE AUR KHUMB

SABAT MASOOR

SPICY BROWN LENTILS

SERVES 4

1 x 400 g can brown lentils
2 T (30 ml) oil
1 onion, minced or grated
2 t (10 ml) garlic paste
½ t (2.5 ml) ginger paste
½ t (2.5 ml) turmeric
1 t (5 ml) paprika
1 t (5 ml) ground cumin
1 t (5 ml) ground coriander
½ t (2.5 ml) garam masala (p 122)
½ green chilli, chopped (optional)
1 large tomato, grated
2 T (30 ml) finely chopped fresh coriander
salt to taste
2 cups (500 ml) hot water
1 t (5 ml) chopped fresh coriander, for garnish

Drain and wash the lentils with fresh water, drain and set aside.

In a deep pan, heat the oil over medium heat. Add the onion and sauté until golden brown. Lower heat. Add the garlic and ginger pastes and stir-fry for 30 seconds. Stir in all the dry spices, green chilli (if using), tomato, 2 T (30 ml) fresh coriander and salt. Stir and cook for 2–3 minutes or until the oil just starts to float. Add the lentils and water and bring to a boil. Reduce heat, cover and simmer for 10 minutes. Remove from heat and mash the lentils with the back of a spoon against the side of the pan to get a mushy texture. Transfer to a serving dish and garnish with 1 t (5 ml) chopped coriander.

Serve hot with any non-vegetarian main dish or tandoori preparation, or a side dish of vegetables, chapati (p 98) or bread rolls, and plain yoghurt or raita (pp 75–79).

SIDE DISHES

YOGHURT AND VEGETABLE

Nutrition pundits the world over are in agreement that our daily food plan should include plenty of fresh vegetables. Apart from being an excellent source of vitamins, minerals and fibre, and low in kilojoules, they add colour, flavour and texture to our menu. Since the majority of the Indian population is vegetarian, there is a wonderful variety of delicious vegetable recipes in Indian cuisine. Vegetables are cooked either with gravy or dry and in different combinations, using different herbs and spices.

A common fault in Indian cooking seems to be a tendency to overcook vegetables, although this is changing as people become more aware of the loss of important nutrients that results from overcooking. Cooked vegetables should not be kept hot after cooking, as this will also destroy heat-sensitive nutrients, but rather be reheated in the microwave or on top of the stove just before serving. Raw vegetables are used in salads or added to yoghurt to make raita.

I have selected recipes using vegetables that should be very familiar to South Africans, readily available and easy to cook.

Apart from the extensive use of yoghurt (dahi) in cooking, no Indian meal is complete without a yoghurt side dish, either in the form of raita – yoghurt mixed with vegetables – or on its own. It provides a cooling contrast to spicy dishes and is a good source of calcium and protein.

I have used low-fat yoghurt in the recipes that follow, but feel free to substitute it with Greek or full-cream yoghurt, or your own home-made yoghurt (p 118). Raita goes particularly well with rice pulao or biryani.

GOBI ALOO
CAULIFLOWER WITH POTATOES
SERVES 4

1 T (15 ml) oil
1 t (5 ml) cumin seeds
1 t (5 ml) finely chopped garlic
1 t (5 ml) finely chopped root ginger
½ t (2.5 ml) turmeric
½ t (2.5 ml) paprika

1 t (5 ml) ground cumin
½ t (2.5 ml) garam masala (p 122)
salt to taste
2 medium potatoes, peeled and cut into small pieces
500 g cauliflower, cut into small florets
1 T (15 ml) chopped fresh coriander

Heat the oil in a wide-based, non-stick pan, over medium heat. Stir in the cumin seeds, garlic and ginger and fry for a minute or until the garlic just starts to change colour. Reduce heat to low and add all the spices, salt and potatoes. Cook covered for 5–7 minutes, stirring occasionally. Add cauliflower and coriander, reduce heat to very low, cover and cook, stirring in between to prevent sticking and burning, until the vegetables are tender.

Serve with any meat or vegetarian main dish, chapati (p 98) or paratha (pp 101–102) and raita (pp 75–79), or with plain yoghurt.

TIP
You can use a sprinkle of water to prevent the vegetables from sticking.

PATTA GOBI AUR MATTAR
CABBAGE WITH PEAS
SERVES 4

4 t (20 ml) oil
1 t (5 ml) cumin seeds
400 g cabbage, shredded
1 tomato, chopped
½ t (2.5 ml) turmeric

½ t (2.5 ml) garam masala (p 122)
½ t (2.5 ml) paprika
salt to taste
1½ cups (375 ml) frozen green peas, thawed

Heat the oil in a wide-based pan over medium heat. Add the cumin and fry for a few seconds or until the cumin starts to change colour. Stir in the cabbage, tomato, spices and salt. Stir and cook for 5 minutes.

Add the peas and continue to stir-fry for 5 minutes, longer or until the cabbage is tender but crunchy and dry. Remove from heat.

Serve with any meat or vegetarian main dish, chapati (p 98) or paratha (pp 101–102) and raita (pp 75–79), or with plain yoghurt.

GOBI ALOO

SABZI AUR CHANNE

SABZI AUR CHANNE

MIXED VEGETABLES WITH CHICKPEAS

SERVES 6–8

2 T (30 ml) tomato purée
1 cup (250 ml) low-fat yoghurt
½ t (2.5 ml) chilli powder
1 t (5 ml) paprika
1 t (5 ml) garam masala
¼ t (1.25 ml) pepper
¼ t (1.25 ml) ground mace
1 t (5 ml) ginger paste
½ t (2.5 ml) salt
1 x 400 g can chickpeas
2 T (30 ml) oil
1 T (15 ml) unsalted butter
1 x 3 cm piece stick cinnamon
2 cardamom pods, cracked
2 bay leaves
2 onions, coarsely chopped
1 t (5 ml) garlic paste
1 potato, peeled and cut into 2 cm cubes
2 cups (500 ml) small cauliflower florets
10 green beans, cut into 2 cm pieces
2 baby marrows, sliced
1 T (15 ml) finely chopped fresh coriander
½ cup (125 ml) hot water, or more if required
salt to taste
¼ cup (60 ml) cream
2 t (10 ml) sesame seeds, roasted, for garnish

Place the tomato purée, yoghurt, all dry ground spices, ginger paste and ½ t (2.5 ml) salt in a mixing bowl and whisk until smooth. Set aside.

Drain and wash the chickpeas, and drain again. Set aside.

Heat the oil and butter in a wok or a deep pan over medium heat. Stir in the cinnamon, cardamom, bay leaves, onions and garlic paste and stir-fry until the onion is golden brown. Stir in the yoghurt mixture and continue to stir and cook until the mixture starts to bubble. Reduce heat to low, cover and simmer for 3–4 minutes. Add all the vegetables, coriander, water and salt to taste. Mix, cover and cook until the vegetables are tender but still crunchy. Stir in the cream and bring the mixture to a boil. Remove from heat, transfer to a serving dish and sprinkle with sesame seeds to garnish.

Serve with any meat or vegetarian main dish, rice and raita (pp 75–79), or plain yoghurt.

PALAK DAAL

PALAK DAAL
SPINACH AND SPLIT PEAS
SERVES 4

¼ cup (60 ml) yellow split peas
2 cups (500 ml) water
½ t (2.5 ml) salt
2 T (30 ml) oil
1 onion, finely chopped
2 t (10 ml) finely chopped garlic
½ t (2.5 ml) ginger paste
1 t (5 ml) ground cumin
1 t (5 ml) paprika
1 t (5 ml) ground coriander
salt to taste
500 g spinach, finely chopped
1 T (15 ml) lemon juice

Pick over and wash the split peas. In a small saucepan, bring the water to a boil. Add ½ t (2.5 ml) salt and the split peas. Lower heat and simmer until the peas are soft but not mushy. Remove from heat and strain. Set aside.
Heat the oil in a wide-based pan over medium heat. Add the onion, garlic and ginger and sauté for 2 minutes or until the onion is translucent. Add all the spices, salt, spinach and lemon juice and mix well.
Cook uncovered for 2 minutes or until the spinach has wilted and the juices have been released. Continue to cook and stir for 5–7 minutes longer or until the spinach is cooked and all the liquid is absorbed. If too much liquid remains, keep the heat on high until the water has evaporated. Stir in the cooked split peas, mix well and cook for another minute.
Serve with any meat or vegetarian main dish, chapati (p 98) or paratha (pp 101–102) and raita (pp 75–79), or with plain yoghurt.

VEGETABLE JALFREZI
DELIGHTFUL MIXED VEGETABLES
SERVES 6–8

Although lentils are not traditionally part of this vegetable dish, I like to use them to enhance the nutritive value, as well as the flavour and texture.

2 T (30 ml) oil
1 t (5 ml) cumin seeds
2 onions, coarsely chopped
1 t (5 ml) red chillies, crushed, or to taste
1½ cups (375 ml) seeded and coarsely chopped green or red pepper (or both)
3 cups (750 ml) coarsely chopped cabbage
1 cup (250 ml) coarsely chopped green beans
1 cup (250 ml) sliced carrots
1 t (5 ml) ginger paste
2 t (10 ml) finely chopped root ginger
½ t (2.5 ml) pepper
1 x 400 g can whole lentils, washed and drained
½ t (2.5 ml) paprika
1 t (5 ml) ground cumin
salt to taste
2 T (30 ml) chopped fresh coriander
5 T (75 ml) tomato purée
1½ T (22.5 ml) white vinegar

Heat the oil in a wide-based pan over medium heat. Add the cumin seeds, onions and crushed chillies and sauté for a minute. Stir in all the remaining ingredients except the tomato purée and vinegar. Reduce the heat, cover and cook for about 10 minutes or until the vegetables are just tender. Stir in the tomato purée and vinegar, mix well and cook for 2 minutes longer. Remove from heat and transfer to a serving dish.
Serve hot with any meat dish or aloo soya tikki (p 17) or balti paneer (p 52) with chapati (p 98) or paratha (pp 101–102).

MASALA BHINDI AUR DAAL

SPICY OKRA WITH YELLOW LENTILS

SERVES 4

¾ cup (180 ml) yellow lentils or yellow split peas
3 cups (750 ml) water
½ t (2.5 ml) salt
2 T (30 ml) oil
1 t (5 ml) cumin seeds, coarsely ground
1 t (5 ml) coriander seeds, coarsely ground
1 large onion, thinly sliced
2 t (10 ml) garlic paste
1 t (5 ml) ginger paste
½ t (2.5 ml) turmeric
½ t (2.5 ml) chilli powder, or to taste
2 t (10 ml) ground coriander
salt to taste
2 t (10 ml) raw mango powder, or
1 T (15 ml) lemon juice
400 g okra, cut into 1 cm pieces
1 large tomato, coarsely chopped

Pick over and wash the lentils or split peas, removing any stones. Place the water and salt in a saucepan and bring to a boil over medium heat. Add the lentils and cook until soft but not mushy. Drain and set aside.
Heat the oil in a wok or any round-bottomed pan over medium heat. Stir in the ground cumin and coriander seeds and fry for 30 seconds. Add the onion and sauté until golden brown in colour. Stir in all the remaining ingredients except for the cooked lentils and tomato. Stir and cook for 5 minutes or until the okra is almost tender. Stir in the cooked lentils and tomatoes and cook for 2 minutes longer. Remove from heat. Transfer to a serving dish. Serve hot with any meat dish or vegetarian main dish, chapati (p 98) and yoghurt raita (pp 75–79) or with plain rice and pudina chutney (p 123).

SABAT SABZIAN BALTI STYLE

STIR-FRIED BABY VEGETABLES

SERVES 6 AS A SIDE DISH OR 4 AS A MAIN DISH

2 T (30 ml) oil
4 small onions or shallots, peeled and halved
1 t (5 ml) garlic paste
1 t (5 ml) ginger paste
½ t (2.5 ml) chilli powder, or to taste
½ t (2.5 ml) paprika
1 t (5 ml) ground cumin
½ t (2.5 ml) garam masala (p 122)
¼ cup (60 ml) tomato purée
8 small baby marrows
8 baby carrots
8 baby corn cobs
½ cup (125 ml) water
8 baby potatoes, cooked and peeled
1 x 400 g can chickpeas, washed and drained
8 cherry tomatoes
salt to taste
4 t (20 ml) sesame seeds

Heat oil in a wok or deep, round-bottomed pan over medium heat. Add onions or shallots, garlic and ginger pastes and stir-fry for about a minute. Add all dry spices and tomato purée, stir and cook for another minute. Stir in the marrows, carrots, corn and water. Cover and cook for 8–10 minutes, or until the vegetables are tender but still crunchy. Stir in the potatoes, chickpeas, tomatoes, salt and 2 t (10 ml) sesame seeds. Stir-fry for 2 minutes or until potatoes are heated through. Remove from heat. Transfer to a serving dish and sprinkle with the remaining sesame seeds.

Serve hot, with any meat dish or vegetarian main dish, chapati (p 98) or rice and home-made yoghurt (p 118), or as a main dish with a salad of your choice and bread for a healthy vegetarian meal.

VARIATION

Any combination of vegetables may be used in place of those suggested above.

BAINGAN BHARTHA

ROASTED EGGPLANT WITH HERBS AND ONIONS

SERVES 6

2 large, firm eggplants
1 T (15 ml) oil
1 T (15 ml) unsalted butter
1 medium onion, chopped
1 t (5 ml) finely chopped root ginger
2 tomatoes, finely chopped
1 cup (250 ml) frozen green peas, thawed
2 T (30 ml) chopped fresh coriander
½ t (2.5 ml) paprika
½ green chilli, seeded and chopped (optional)
salt to taste

Smear the eggplants with a little oil and roast them under a hot grill until they are soft and the outer skin is wrinkled and charred. Place under a running tap and peel off the skin. Remove the stems and mash the eggplants, in a plate, with a potato masher or fork, into a smooth, paste-like consistency. Set aside.

Heat the oil and butter in a frying pan over medium heat. Add the onion and ginger. Sauté for a minute and stir in all the remaining ingredients except for the eggplant paste. Stir-fry for 2 minutes. Add the eggplant and continue to stir-fry for another 2 minutes. Remove from heat and transfer to a serving dish.

Serve hot with any meat dish or vegetarian main dish, paratha (pp 101–102) and yoghurt raita (pp 75–79) or plain yoghurt.

ANGOOR AUR AKHROT RAITA

YOGHURT WITH GRAPES AND WALNUTS

SERVES 4

2 cups (500 ml) low-fat yoghurt
½ t (2.5 ml) ground cumin
½ t (2.5 ml) pepper
½ t (2.5 ml) chilli powder (optional)
1 t (5 ml) sugar
salt to taste
¾ cup (180 ml) seedless grapes, cut in half
¼ cup (60 ml) coarsely chopped walnuts
pinch of chilli powder, for garnish

Beat the yoghurt, spices, sugar and salt in a bowl with a fork or hand mixer until smooth and creamy. Add the grapes and walnuts, saving 1 t (5 ml) of walnuts for garnish. Mix well and sprinkle with a pinch of chilli powder and reserved walnuts. Serve chilled.

KHEERA PUDINA RAITA

YOGHURT WITH CUCUMBER AND MINT

SERVES 4

2 cups (500 ml) low-fat yoghurt
½ t (2.5 ml) roasted ground cumin (p 122)
½ t (2.5 ml) ground cumin
¼ t (1.25 ml) chilli powder
1 green chilli, seeded and finely chopped (optional)
¼ t (1.25 ml) pepper
1 t (5 ml) sugar
salt to taste
¾ cup (180 ml) peeled and grated cucumber
1½ T (22.5 ml) chopped mint leaves
pinch each of roasted ground cumin and chilli powder, for garnish

Beat the yoghurt, spices, sugar and salt in a bowl with a fork or hand beater until smooth and creamy. Stir in the cucumber and mint, saving some mint. Sprinkle with a pinch each of roasted ground cumin and chilli powder and reserved mint. Serve chilled.

BAINGAN KA RAITA

YOGHURT WITH EGGPLANT

SERVES 4

1 small eggplant
2 cups (500 ml) low-fat yoghurt
1 t (5 ml) ground coriander
½ t (2.5 ml) pepper
½ t (2.5 ml) paprika
salt to taste
2 small spring onions, finely chopped, with greens
1 T (15 ml) finely chopped fresh coriander
a little chilli powder, for garnish

Roast the whole eggplant under a preheated grill until soft and skin is charred almost black. Cool under a running tap and peel off the skin. Mash the pulp into a fine paste. Set aside.
Place the yoghurt, spices and salt in a bowl. Beat with a fork or hand beater until smooth and creamy. Stir in eggplant pulp, onions and coriander. Mix thoroughly. Serve chilled, sprinkled with a little chilli powder.

PALAK RAITA

YOGHURT WITH SPINACH

SERVES 4

sprinkling of water
¼ t (1.25 ml) salt
1½ cups (375 ml) finely chopped spinach, washed
2 cups (500 ml) low-fat yoghurt
1 t (5 ml) finely chopped fresh dill
½ t (2.5 ml) ginger paste
½ t (2.5 ml) roasted ground cumin (p 122)
1 t (5 ml) ground cumin
2 t (10 ml) white sugar
salt to taste
a little chilli powder, for garnish
a little roasted ground cumin, for garnish

Place a small pan over medium heat and add a sprinkle of water and ¼ t (1.25 ml) of salt. Add the spinach and stir well. Cook for a minute or until the spinach has wilted. Increase heat and continue cooking uncovered until the water has evaporated. Remove from heat and let it cool.

Place the remaining ingredients, except the garnishes, in a bowl and beat with a fork or hand beater until smooth and creamy. Add the spinach and mix thoroughly. Serve chilled, sprinkled with a little chilli powder and roasted ground cumin.

PALAK RAITA

BAINGAN KA RAITA

KACHOOMBER RAITA

MIXED VEGETABLES IN YOGHURT

SERVES 4

2 cups (500 ml) low-fat yoghurt
½ t (2.5 ml) roasted ground cumin (p 122)
1 t (5 ml) ground cumin
½ t (2.5 ml) pepper
½ t (2.5 ml) paprika
1 t (5 ml) grated lemon rind
¼ cup (60 ml) finely chopped cucumber
¼ cup (60 ml) chopped tomato
1 cup (250 ml) chopped crisp lettuce
1 T (15 ml) finely chopped onion
1 T (15 ml) finely chopped mint leaves
salt to taste
paprika or roasted ground cumin, for garnish

Place the yoghurt, all the spices and the lemon rind in a bowl and whisk to mix. Stir in all the vegetables and salt. Garnish with a little paprika or roasted ground cumin. Serve chilled.

VARIATION
Substitute the cucumber, tomato and lettuce with 1½ cups (375 ml) of finely diced cooked potato and you have a delicious aloo (potato) raita, slightly different from the recipe below.

ALOO RAITA

YOGHURT WITH POTATOES

SERVES 4

2 cups (500 ml) low-fat yoghurt
½ t (2.5 ml) roasted ground cumin (p 122)
½ t (2.5 ml) ground cumin
½ t (2.5 ml) pepper
salt to taste
1 T (15 ml) finely chopped mint leaves
2 T (30 ml) finely chopped spring onion
2 medium potatoes, cut into small pieces
1 small green chilli, seeded and finely chopped (optional)
paprika or chilli powder, for garnish

Place the yoghurt, cumin, pepper, salt and mint leaves in a mixing bowl and whisk. Stir in all the remaining ingredients, except the garnish. Adjust the seasoning. Transfer to a serving bowl and garnish with a dusting of paprika or chilli powder. Serve chilled.

ALOO RAITA (TOP) AND
KACHOOMBER RAITA (BOTTOM)

No Indian meal is considered complete without either rice or bread (chapati, roti or naan) in the menu. In northern India, wheat forms the basis of the meal, while in the south it is rice. From a nutritional point of view, cereals (usually rice and wheat) form the major part of our diet, providing on average 55 to 60% of our total daily kilojoule requirements and the energy required for important bodily functions.

There are different varieties of rice available in India, and different types suit different dishes. The best variety available, and the most highly regarded, is basmati, which is mainly used for pulao and biryani. It has long, slender grains and a fragrant aroma. Round, short-grained rice and parboiled rice are more commonly used.

The quality of any rice improves with age, especially that of basmati. Freshly harvested rice becomes starchy and does not increase in volume when cooked as much as rice that has been stored for a year or more. The aroma and flavour also improve with age and storage.

re cooking rice, always wash it gently but thoroughly in a colander or sieve

running water until the water runs clear. This removes starch particles and

es the texture of the cooked rice. To half-cook rice, for those recipes that

it, press a grain or two between your thumb and index finger – the rice

be soft on top and hard in the middle.

most popular rice preparations are plain boiled, pulao and biryani.

RICE
DISHES

BOILED RICE

The rice is simply cooked in lightly salted, boiling water. When it is cooked, it is drained and served with cooked pulses and legumes, or fish, meat or vegetable preparations. Southern Indians generally serve boiled rice at every meal, whereas northern Indians will serve it very occasionally, for example with punjabi rajma.

RICE PULAO

Pulao was introduced to India by the Moghuls and today it is more popular in the northern parts of India than in the south. It is basically a combination of rice and meat or chicken, vegetables or legumes, with various spices, cooked in a tightly covered pan over low heat with just enough water to be absorbed by the rice. Different types of pulao are prepared for festive occasions and holidays.

Only the best-quality rice should be used for preparing pulao. It can be served as a main dish along with raita (yoghurt side dish) and chutney. Vegetable pulao goes very well with roast lamb, grilled chops or beef steak.

Pulao freezes well and can be heated in the microwave before serving. It will keep fresh for 2–3 days in the refrigerator.

SABZI KI BIRYANI

BIRYANI

Like pulao, biryani was brought to India by the Moghuls. It is a very attractive, elegant dish prepared for special occasions. Though usually cooked with meat, chicken or fish, the vegetarian version uses cauliflower, beans, carrots, peas, nuts and fruits, and is equally wonderful.

The cooking method is different to that of pulao and more time consuming. Partially cooked rice and meat or vegetables are layered in a heavy, flat-bottomed pan and then cooked. Traditionally, biryani should be cooked over very slow heat in a pot with a tight lid and sealed with flour dough to contain the steam and aromas. I use an easier method, however; after layering I cover the pot first with foil and then place the lid on tightly. It can either be cooked on top of the stove or baked in the oven after layering.

One of the most important ingredients used in biryani is saffron soaked in warm milk, which is drizzled over the rice at the time of layering. Saffron partly colours some of the rice grains orange and also gives a very distinctive aroma to biryani. Though used in tiny amounts, saffron is a very expensive spice and not easily available, except from some grocery stores and Indian grocers. As a substitute, a little yellow food colouring diluted with a little water will serve the purpose, although the delicate flavour of saffron will be lacking.

I have used basmati rice in my recipes, which is easily available under various brand names. If it is not available, use any good-quality, long-grain rice instead.

Do not be put off by the long list of ingredients for biryani and what seems to be a laborious method of cooking. Once you have assembled all the ingredients and read the method carefully, you will really enjoy making it and the joy of eating it with your family or friends will make your effort more than worthwhile.

Always use a heavy-bottomed, flat pan for preparing recipes in this section.

MATTAR PULAO

KHUMB WALA PULAO

MATTAR PULAO

RICE WITH GREEN PEAS

SERVES 4

4 t (20 ml) oil
2 bay leaves
2 cardamom pods, cracked
1 medium onion, thinly sliced
½ t (2.5 ml) cumin seeds
2¾ cups (680 ml) water
1½ cups (375 ml) frozen green peas, thawed
1½ cups (375 ml) basmati rice, washed and drained
1½ t (7.5 ml) salt, or to taste

Heat the oil in a pan over medium heat. Stir in the bay leaves and cardamom and fry for 30 seconds. Add the onion and cumin seeds and stir-fry until golden brown. Add the water, bring to a boil and stir in the peas, rice and salt. Bring to a boil again, cover and cook for 5 minutes. Reduce heat to low and cook for another 10–15 minutes or until the water is completely absorbed and the rice is cooked.
Remove from heat and fluff gently with a fork to separate the grains. Cover and let it stand for 5 minutes before serving.
Serve with any raita or daal of your choice, with any meat dish and a green salad.
This dish goes well with any grilled meat, meat stew or roast.

TIP

Pulao can be prepared in advance and heated, either in the microwave, or in a preheated oven at 190 °C for 15–20 minutes, before serving.

KHUMB WALA PULAO

RICE WITH MUSHROOMS

SERVES 4

4 t (20 ml) oil
1 x 2 cm piece stick cinnamon
2 cardamom pods, cracked
2 bay leaves
4 whole cloves
1 medium onion, thinly sliced
100 g mushrooms, sliced
2½ cups (625 ml) water
1½ cups (375 ml) basmati rice, washed and drained
1½ t (7.5 ml) salt, or to taste

Heat the oil in a pan over medium heat. Stir in the cinnamon, cardamom, bay leaves and cloves and fry for 30 seconds. Add the onion and stir-fry until golden brown. Add the mushrooms and sauté for 5 minutes. Add the water and bring to a boil. Stir in the rice and salt. Bring to a boil again, cover and cook for 5 minutes.
Reduce heat to low and cook for another 7–10 minutes or until the water is absorbed completely and the rice is cooked. Remove from heat and fluff gently with a fork to separate the grains. Cover and let it stand for 5 minutes before serving. Discard whole spices.
Serve with any raita or daal, with any meat preparation of your choice and a green salad.
This dish goes well with any grilled meat or meat stew or roast.

TIP

Pulao can be prepared in advance and heated, either in the microwave, or in a preheated oven at 190 °C for 15–20 minutes, before serving.

SOYA AUR SABZI PULAO

SOYA AND VEGETABLE RICE

SERVES 6

¾ cup (180 ml) dry soya granules
2 T (30 ml) oil
1 onion, finely chopped
1 t (5 ml) ginger paste
1 t (5 ml) garlic paste
½ t (2.5 ml) turmeric
½ t (2.5 ml) chilli powder or paprika
2 t (10 ml) salt, or to taste
1 t (5 ml) ground cumin
1 t (5 ml) garam masala (p 122)
2 medium tomatoes, chopped
3½ cups (875 ml) water
1 cup (250 ml) small cauliflower florets
1 cup (250 ml) sliced carrots
1½ cups (375 ml) basmati rice, washed and drained
2 T (30 ml) lemon juice

Prepare soya granules (see page 120). Set aside.
Heat the oil in a pan over medium heat. Add the
onion and sauté until golden brown. Stir in the
ginger and garlic pastes, all the dry spices and
tomatoes. Stir-fry for a minute. Add the prepared
soya granules and stir-fry for 2–3 minutes longer.
Add the water and bring to a boil.
Cover and cook for 5 minutes.
Stir in the vegetables, rice and lemon juice. Bring
to a boil again, cover, reduce heat to low, and
continue cooking for 15–20 minutes or until the rice
is cooked and the water is absorbed. Remove from
heat, fluff with a fork and let it stand for 5 minutes
before serving.
This dish makes a healthy and nutritious meal by
itself, especially for vegetarians, but to enhance the
nutritive value further, serve it with a small bowl of
plain yoghurt and a green salad.

TIP

Pulao can be prepared in advance and heated, in a
microwave, or in a preheated oven at 190 °C for
15–20 minutes, just before serving.

YAKHNI PULAO

RICE COOKED IN RICH STOCK AND MILK

SERVES 6

1 cup (250 ml) (or more) low-fat milk
2 T (30 ml) oil
1 medium onion, finely chopped
1 t (5 ml) finely chopped garlic
1 t (5 ml) finely chopped root ginger
2 cups (500 ml) basmati rice, washed and drained
yakhni (stock)
800 g small lamb chops
4 cups (1 litre) water
1 x 2.5 cm piece stick cinnamon
3 cardamom pods, cracked
4 whole cloves
6 whole peppercorns
3 bay leaves
2 medium onions, coarsely chopped
1 t (5 ml) coarsely chopped garlic
2 t (10 ml) salt, or to taste

First make the stock: place all the ingredients in a
heavy pan and bring to a boil over medium heat.
Reduce heat and cook for about 45 minutes or until
the meat is cooked. Strain and discard all whole
spices. Remove the meat from the stock, debone
and set aside. Add enough milk to the stock to
make up 4 cups (1 litre) of liquid. Set aside.
Heat the oil in a pan over medium heat. Add the
onion, garlic and ginger and sauté until golden.
Add the cooked meat and stir-fry for 5–7 minutes.
Add the milk and stock mixture, and rice and bring
to a boil. Cover and cook for 5–7 minutes.
Reduce heat to low and cook covered for another
15 minutes or until the liquid is fully absorbed and
the rice is cooked. Remove from heat and let the
pulao stand for 10 minutes. Fluff with a fork.
Serve with plain yoghurt and pudina chutney
(p 123).

TIP

Yakhni pulao can be prepared in advance and
heated, in a microwave, or in a preheated oven
at 190 °C for 15–20 minutes, before serving.

YAKHNI PULAO

HARA PULAO

HARA PULAO

RICE WITH GREEN HERBS

SERVES 4

2 T (30 ml) oil
1 medium onion, finely chopped
½ t (2.5 ml) ginger paste
½ t (2.5 ml) garlic paste
salt to taste
2 T (30 ml) minced fresh coriander
1 T (15 ml) minced mint leaves
2½ cups (625 ml) water
2 T (30 ml) low-fat yoghurt, well whisked
1½ cups (375 ml) basmati rice, washed and drained

Heat the oil in a pan over medium heat. Add the onion and stir-fry until golden brown. Add the ginger and garlic pastes, salt, coriander and mint and sauté for 30 seconds. Add the water and yoghurt and bring to a boil. Stir in the rice. Bring to a boil again, cover and cook for 5 minutes.

Reduce heat to low and cook for another 7–10 minutes or until the water is absorbed completely and the rice is cooked. Remove from heat, fluff gently with a fork to separate the grains. Cover and let it stand for 5 minutes before serving.

Serve with any lamb dish or vegetarian main dish, accompanied by a vegetable or yoghurt side dish.

This dish goes well with a lamb or beef roast, grilled lamb chops or fish.

TIP
Hara pulao can be prepared in advance and heated, in a microwave, or in a preheated oven at 190 °C for 15–20 minutes, before serving.

SABZI KI BIRYANI

VEGETABLE BIRYANI

SERVES 6

2 cups (500 ml) basmati rice
a few saffron strands, crushed (or 3–4 drops yellow
food colouring if saffron is not available)
2 T (30 ml) hot milk
¾ cup (180 ml) low-fat yoghurt
2 t (10 ml) garlic paste
1 t (5 ml) ginger paste
1 t (5 ml) ground cumin
½ t (2.5 ml) chilli powder, or to taste
1 t (5 ml) garam masala (p 122)
2 T (30 ml) ground almonds
1 T (15 ml) cooking oil
2 T (30 ml) unsalted butter
2 medium onions, thinly sliced
4 whole cloves

2 bay leaves
1 x 2 cm piece stick cinnamon
3 cardamom pods, cracked
4 whole peppercorns
1 green chilli, chopped (optional)
1 cup (250 ml) cauliflower florets
1 cup (250 ml) sliced carrots
¾ cup (180 ml) frozen green peas, thawed
1 cup (250 ml) green beans, cut into 2 cm pieces
1 T (15 ml) cashew nuts
2 T (30 ml) raisins
salt to taste
2 T (30 ml) chopped fresh coriander
melted butter, for greasing the pan

Boil the rice in sufficient boiling water with a little salt until half cooked (see page 81). Drain thoroughly. Transfer to a mixing bowl and let it cool. Soak the crushed saffron in hot milk and set aside.

Place the yoghurt, garlic and ginger pastes, ground cumin and chilli powder, garam masala and ground almonds in a mixing bowl and beat thoroughly. Set aside.

Heat the oil and butter in a pan over medium heat. Add the onions and fry until golden brown. Lower the heat and remove half the browned onion with a slotted spoon and place it in a small bowl.

Add all the whole spices to the remaining fried onions in the pan and stir-fry for 30 seconds. Stir in the green chilli if using, all the vegetables, cashew nuts, raisins and salt. Increase the heat to medium and stir-fry for about 5 minutes. Stir in the yoghurt mixture and bring to a boil. Reduce the heat and continue to stir-fry for 8–10 minutes. Remove from heat and set aside.

Mix together the reserved fried onion and coriander and set aside. Grease a pan with melted butter and evenly spread half the cooked rice in it. Pour over the vegetable mixture, and then spread the onion and coriander mixture over. Cover with the remaining rice and sprinkle with the milk and saffron mixture. Cover first with foil and then with a tight lid. Cook over medium low heat for about 10–15 minutes. Remove from heat and let it stand for 20 minutes. Before serving, mix gently with a fork, transfer to a platter and garnish with fried onions and coriander.

Serve with kachoomber raita (p 79) and you have a perfect meal.

Another attractive way to serve it is to unmould the biryani on a platter and garnish.

FOR BAKING
Preheat the oven to 200 °C.
Grease the bottom of a suitable baking dish with melted butter and layer the rice and vegetables as above. Cover first with foil and then with a tight-fitting lid. Bake for about 15–20 minutes and serve as suggested above.

GOSHT BIRYANI

MEAT BIRYANI

SERVES 6

750 g lamb, boned and cut into small cubes
enough oil to fry onions
2 medium onions, finely sliced
2 T (30 ml) raisins
2 T (30 ml) blanched slivered almonds
1 t (5 ml) saffron strands, crushed
2 T (30 ml) hot milk
2½ cups (625 ml) basmati rice, washed and drained
1 t (5 ml) salt, or to taste
1 large onion, coarsely chopped
3–4 cloves garlic, chopped
1 t (5 ml) chopped root ginger
3 T (45 ml) water
1 T (15 ml) oil (from same oil used for frying)
2 T (30 ml) butter

1 x 2 cm piece stick cinnamon
½ t (2.5 ml) cardamom seeds
½ t (2.5 ml) whole peppercorns
2 t (10 ml) cumin seeds
2 t (10 ml) coriander seeds
pinch of grated nutmeg
1 hard-boiled egg, shelled and sliced

marinade

1 cup (250 ml) low-fat yoghurt, well whisked
2 t (10 ml) garlic paste
1 t (5 ml) ginger paste
meat tenderiser, quantity as per label instructions
1½ t (7.5 ml) salt or to taste
1 t (5 ml) chilli powder or paprika

Place the lamb, with all the marinade ingredients in a mixing bowl and combine thoroughly. Cover and let it marinate for at least an hour.

Heat enough oil in a wok or pan over medium heat and fry the sliced onions until golden brown and crisp. Remove with a slotted spoon and spread on paper towel. To the same oil, add the raisins and remove them as soon as they swell (almost immediately) and place on kitchen paper towel. Fry half the slivered almonds for a few seconds until golden and place on kitchen paper towel. Remove oil from heat. Soak the saffron in hot milk and set aside. Cook the rice in sufficient water until half cooked. Drain, then spread it on a large platter and sprinkle with a little salt.

Blend the chopped onion, garlic, ginger, remaining slivered almonds and 3 T (45 ml) of water until smooth. Heat the oil and butter in a heavy-bottomed pan over medium heat. Add the whole spices and seeds and sauté for 10 seconds. Add onion and almond mixture and stir-fry until golden brown. If the onion sticks, sprinkle with a little water and continue stir-frying. Stir in the marinated lamb and nutmeg, stir and cook until it starts to bubble. Reduce heat to low, cover the pan tightly and let it cook for 45–60 minutes or until the lamb is tender and about a cup of sauce remains. Remove from heat. Preheat the oven to 150 °C.

To layer the biryani, use an ovenproof dish with a tight-fitting lid. Spoon some sauce from the cooked lamb into the bottom of the dish. Next, spread half the cooked rice and top it with cooked lamb with the sauce. Sprinkle fried onions over (saving a little for garnish) and top with the remaining rice. Spoon the saffron mixture over the rice. Cover the dish first with foil and then the lid. Bake in the middle of the oven for an hour. Remove from oven and let it stand for a few minutes. Before serving, gently stir the biryani. Serve on a platter, garnished with sliced egg, fried raisins, almonds and onions.

Serve with tarka daal (p 59) and kachoomber raita (p 79).

TIP

This dish can be prepared a day or two in advance, up to the layering stage and refrigerated. Bake when required. Chicken (without tenderiser), beef or veal may be used instead of lamb.

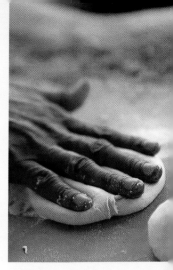

BREADS

Bread is an essential part of an Indian meal, particularly in the north. There are several different types

of bread, mostly unleavened (without yeast).

Most Indian breads are made with very finely ground, wholewheat flour known as atta, and

are cooked on a tawa (a concave, heavy iron plate) or griddle, or deep fried or baked in a

tandoor (clay oven).

Unfortunately I have not been able to find a really good substitute for Indian atta in Johannesburg.

I have tried using wheat-meal (wholewheat) flour, but the bread has not been as soft as that made

with atta. By experimenting with a combination of finely sifted wheat-meal (wholewheat) flour and all-

purpose flour (cake flour), I have had better results, with the bread being much softer and better-looking.

Naturally some of the vital nutrients are lost without the proper flour, and if you do have access to an

Indian provision store, it is advisable to buy roti atta or roti flour.

BREADS

POORI

The dough for pooris is harder in consistency than that for chapatis and parathas, and a little oil or ghee is added to the flour. Poori is also generally smaller in size and rolled slightly thicker. It is deep fried in hot oil and should puff up into small, crisp balls, although they are quite soft when eaten and taste best when hot. We fry pooris in a karahi – an Indian version of a wok – but any suitable deep saucepan may be used. The rolled pooris are covered with a damp cloth, wax paper or clingfilm to prevent them from drying out before cooking. Once the oil is hot, they can be fried very quickly.

CHAPATI (Also known as roti or phulka)

This everyday bread, eaten by most Indians, is the thinnest of the breads. It takes a little practice to make reasonably decent chapatis! The dough is made simply with flour and water, sometimes with a little salt added to the flour. The dough should be soft but not sticky, which makes rolling much easier (use extra flour while rolling to avoid sticking).

A tawa is traditionally used for making chapatis, but you can use a griddle or heavy frying pan for the purpose. The chapati is first toasted on both sides over a pre-heated tawa/griddle/frying pan and then 'inflated' directly over burning charcoal or a gas burner. Chapatis taste best straight off the fire, although this is of course not always possible. At my home in Johannesburg, I stack chapatis one on top of the other, then wrap 6 to 10 of them in clingfilm and freeze them for later use. Microwaved or heated in the oven when required, they taste as good as fresh. Some like to spread them with a little butter or ghee as soon as they are made.

PARATHA

Like chapati, this is an unleavened bread, but it is shallow fried and has rich, flaky layers. Traditionally a little oil, butter or ghee is added to the flour before making the dough, although I omit this to cut down on fat and unnecessary kilojoules.

Parathas are surprisingly easy to make at home. The dough is made in the same way as for chapatis, although unlike a chapati, a paratha can be rolled into different shapes, such as triangles, squares or circles, and is slightly thicker than a chapati. It is cooked in the same way as a chapati, but a little oil or ghee is applied to both sides while cooking.

Parathas can be frozen and reheated. They are occasionally served in place of chapatis, or at breakfast with fried eggs, raita or plain yoghurt.

NAAN

Naan is a leavened flat bread from northern India, made with cake flour. Traditionally, it is baked in a very hot tandoor (clay oven), but these are restricted to restaurants now. I cook naan in a conventional oven and under the grill, and the result is fairly acceptable. There are different recipes and methods for making naan. The method that I use (p 105), is easy to follow and the result is quite authentic.

Naan can be served with any vegetarian or meat dish, especially tandoori specialties.

TIPS FOR MAKING INDIAN BREAD

1. Sieve the flour before measuring it.
2. Do not add all the water at once. The amount of water may have to be adjusted a little depending on the type of flour you are using.
3. We generally knead bread dough by hand, but a food processor may be used instead.
4. Always make sure that the tawa or griddle is not so hot that it burns the bread. It is advisable to keep the heat on the low side rather than too high. Chapatis and parathas cook very fast and need to be turned about 3 times.
5. Always rest the dough for about half an hour before rolling.
6. Roll chapatis, parathas or pooris first, spread them over the counter without overlapping and cover them with a damp kitchen towel to prevent them from drying out before cooking.
7. Stack cooked chapatis or parathas as they are made and wrap them in a napkin if they are to be eaten the same day, or in foil or clingfilm for later. They freeze well and stay fresh for months.

POORI
DEEP-FRIED BREAD
MAKES 16

1⅓ cups (330 ml) roti flour (wholewheat flour)
1⅓ cups (330 ml) cake flour
½ t (2.5 ml) salt
1 T (15 ml) oil

¾ cup (180 ml) cold water
¼ cup (60 ml) flour, for dusting
oil for deep frying

Combine the flours, salt and oil in a mixing bowl and rub in well. Gradually add the cold water and knead the dough to a hard consistency. Knead for 5 minutes more, cover with a damp kitchen towel or clingfilm and let the dough rest for 30–40 minutes, or longer.

Divide the dough into 16 equal portions and shape each into a small ball. Work with one portion at a time, keeping the rest covered with a damp cloth or clingfilm. Take one ball, flatten it slightly with your fingertips and roll it out on a floured pastry board with a rolling pin. Dust as required with flour to avoid sticking. Each rolled poori should be about 6–7 cm in diameter. Roll all the pooris, spread them over the counter and cover with a damp kitchen towel to prevent them from drying out.

Heat sufficient oil in a deep frying pan or wok over medium high heat. It is important that the oil is really hot before you start frying the pooris. Drop one poori at a time into the hot oil. As it comes up, turn it over immediately and keep pressing it down to puff it up. (The whole process of frying only takes a few seconds.) The fried poori should be a nice golden colour. Lift the poori out with a slotted spoon, and allow the oil to drain off.

Place on a platter lined with kitchen paper towel to absorb any excess oil. Fry all the pooris in the same way and place on the platter without stacking.

Pooris taste best when served hot and are mostly served with vegetarian dishes.

CHAPATI

PLAIN FLAT BREAD

MAKES 15

2 cups (500 ml) roti flour (wholewheat flour)
½ cup (125 ml) cake flour
a pinch of salt

1 cup (250 ml) warm water
¼ cup (60 ml) flour, for dusting

In a mixing bowl, place the roti flour, cake flour and salt in a heap. Make a well in the centre and gradually add the warm water (1–2 T [15–30 ml] at a time) while stirring from the centre, kneading well to make a soft and pliable dough that leaves the pan clean. Cover the dough with a damp kitchen towel or clingfilm and let it rest for 30–40 minutes. Knead again with moist hands for a couple of minutes. The dough should now spring back when pressed with a finger. Divide the dough into 15 equal portions and shape each one into a round ball. Work with one at a time, while keeping the rest covered with a damp cloth or clingfilm. Take one ball, flatten it slightly with your fingertips and roll it out on a floured pastry board with a rolling pin. Dust frequently with flour to avoid sticking. Each rolled chapati should be about 12–14 cm in diameter. Spread the rolled chapatis on the counter as you go along, covering them with a damp kitchen towel to prevent them from drying out.

Place a griddle or frying pan over medium low heat for 5–7 minutes, and then turn the heat to low. Pick up a rolled chapati, shake off any excess flour, and place it on the preheated griddle or frying pan. Cook until the underside is dry and develops small white spots and small blisters start appearing on the top. Turn the chapati over and cook on the other side until golden brown spots appear. Turn again, pressing the outer edge with a folded cloth, and it should start to inflate. Very gently press the centre down and the chapati should inflate into puffed bread. If this does not happen, please do not panic! It will come with a little practice. A cooked chapati that has not inflated tastes just as good!

Repeat the same procedure with the remaining chapatis, wiping the griddle or frying pan in between to remove any burnt flour. If you wish, you may put a little butter on top of each chapati as soon as it is made, then stack and store them (see point 7 on p 96).

TIKONA PARATHA

TRIANGULAR LAYERED FLAT BREAD

MAKES 12

1½ cups (375 ml) roti flour (wholewheat flour)
1 cup (250 ml) cake flour
½ t (2.5 ml) salt

¼ cup (60 ml) oil or melted butter
1 cup (250 ml) warm water
¼ cup (60 ml) flour, for dusting

In a mixing bowl, place the roti flour, cake flour, salt and 1 T (15 ml) of oil or melted butter and mix with your fingertips until the mixture resembles fine breadcrumbs. Make a well in the centre and gradually add 1–2 T (15–30 ml) of warm water at a time while stirring from the centre, kneading well to make a soft and pliable dough that leaves the bowl clean. Let the dough rest for 30–40 minutes.

Knead again with moist hands for a couple of minutes. The dough should now spring back when pressed with a finger. Divide into 12 equal portions and shape each one into a round ball. Work with one portion at a time, keeping the rest covered with a damp cloth or clingfilm. Take one round, flatten it slightly with your fingertips and roll it out on a floured pastry board with a rolling pin. Dust frequently with flour to prevent sticking. Each rolled paratha should be about 10–12 cm in diameter.

Using a pastry brush, sparingly apply oil or melted butter onto the surface, sprinkle with a little dry flour and fold in half. Apply a little more oil or melted butter onto the surface of the folded paratha, sprinkle with a little more dry flour and fold in half again to form a small triangle. Roll this triangle into a thin, larger triangle, dusting with flour as required. Make all the parathas the same way, spread them over the counter and cover with a damp kitchen towel to prevent them from drying out before cooking.

Place a griddle or frying pan over medium low heat for 5–7 minutes, then turn the heat to low and smear the surface with a little oil or melted butter. Place a paratha on it and brush the top with oil or melted butter. When light brown spots develop on the underside, turn the paratha over and cook until more brown spots appear. The whole process takes about 2–3 minutes.

Place the cooked paratha on a plate and cover with aluminum foil. Cook all the remaining parathas in the same way and stack them under the aluminum foil. If they are not to be eaten immediately, wrap them in aluminum foil or clingfilm. When you are ready to eat, unwrap them and warm them either in a preheated oven at 200 °C for 10–15 minutes or in a microwave.

SOYA PARATHA
FLAT BREAD WITH SOYA GRANULES
MAKES 8

½ cup (125 ml) dry soya granules
2 T (30 ml) oil
1 medium onion, finely chopped
1 T (15 ml) finely chopped root ginger
1 green chilli, seeded and finely chopped (optional)
1 t (5 ml) cumin seeds
1 t (5 ml) ground cumin
1 t (5 ml) ground coriander
1 T (15 ml) finely chopped fresh dill

3 T (45 ml) finely chopped fresh coriander
½ t (2.5 ml) garam masala (p 122)
salt to taste
2 T (30 ml) lemon juice
1 cup (250 ml) roti flour (wholewheat flour)
½ cup (125 ml) cake flour
warm water for making dough
extra flour for dusting
oil for brushing parathas

Prepare soya granules (see page 120). Set aside. Heat the oil in a pan over medium heat. Add the onion, ginger, green chilli if using, and cumin seeds. Sauté for 1 minute. Stir in the prepared soya granules and stir and cook for 2–3 minutes. Add all the ingredients except the flours, water and oil and mix well. Turn off the heat.

Add both the flours to a mixing bowl and mix thoroughly. Make a well in the centre and gradually add the warm water (1–2 T [15–30 ml] at a time) while stirring from the centre, kneading well to make a soft and pliable dough that leaves the pan clean. Cover the dough with a damp kitchen towel or clingfilm and let it rest for 30–40 minutes.

Knead again with moist hands for a couple of minutes. Divide the dough into 16 equal portions and shape each into a round ball. Two portions will be used to make 1 paratha. Roll out 2 separate rounds at a time, like the chapati about 6–8 cm in diameter. Divide the soya mixture into 8 equal portions. Evenly spread one portion of the mixture onto one of the rolled rounds, leaving just

1 cm around the edge clear. Place the other round on top of the filling. Press the edges together to seal the filling inside. Roll out to 12–15 cm diameter, dusting frquently with flour to prevent sticking. Repeat the same with the remaining parathas.

Place a griddle or frying pan over medium low heat for 5–7 minutes, then turn the heat to low and smear the surface with a little oil. Place the paratha on it and brush the top with oil. When light brown spots develop on the underside, turn the paratha over and cook until brown spots appear on the other side as well. The whole process takes about 2–3 minutes.

Place the cooked paratha on a plate and cover with aluminum foil. Cook all the remaining parathas in the same way and stack them under the aluminum foil. If they are not to be eaten immediately, wrap them in aluminum foil or clingfilm. When you are ready to eat, warm them either in a preheated oven at 200 °C for 10–15 minutes or in a microwave.

VARIATION
To cut down further on fat, cook parathas like chapati, without using any oil while cooking.

SOYA PARATHA

NAAN

LEAVENED BREAD

MAKES 8 LARGE NAANS

2½ t (12.5 ml) dried yeast
4 T (60 ml) warm water
2 t (10 ml) sugar
⅔ cup (160 ml) milk, at room temperature
⅔ cup + 2 T (190 ml) low-fat yoghurt, whisked
1 egg, beaten*
2 T (30 ml) melted, unsalted butter

4½ cups (540 g) cake flour
1 t (5 ml) baking powder
½ t (2.5 ml) salt
extra flour for dusting
2 T (30 ml) oil
2 t (10 ml) poppy seeds

Mix the yeast, warm water and sugar in a bowl and let it stand for 3–4 minutes until it becomes frothy. Mix together the milk, yoghurt, egg and melted butter and set aside. In a separate mixing bowl sieve together the flour, baking powder and salt. Make a well in the centre and add the yeast and the milk and yoghurt mixture. Fold in all the ingredients and then knead it until smooth. Cover the bowl tightly with foil or clingfilm and place it in a warm place for 45 minutes to 1 hour, or until the dough has almost doubled its initial volume.
Preheat the oven to 200 °C.

Divide the dough into 8 equal portions and shape each one into a round ball. Work with one portion at a time, keeping the rest covered with a damp cloth or clingfilm. Take one round, flatten it slightly with your fingertips and roll it out on a floured pastry board with a rolling pin. Pull one edge to give the naan a tear shape, which should be about 24 cm long and about 15 cm wide at the widest point. Brush the top surface with a little oil or melted butter, sprinkle with a few poppy seeds and place on a greased baking tray. Roll all the naans and bake in the preheated oven for 10–12 minutes. Wrap in napkins to keep warm and serve hot.
To store them for longer, see point 7 on p 96.

*4 T (60 ml) of extra yoghurt may be substituted for the egg.

FOR THE SWEET TOOTH

I find Indian sweets and desserts rich and time consuming to prepare, and tend not to serve them with daily meals. Instead, meals can be rounded off with seasonal fresh fruits, of which there is an unlimited variety in India. For the kilojoule conscious, it is also best to serve fresh fruit and save sweet indulgences for special occasions only.

Desserts are served at religious functions, weddings and other festive events. Fortunately, there is a huge variety of sweets readily available at 'halvai' (sweetmeat) shops in India and it is not necessary to spend hours making them.

Most desserts are milk-based, with generous use of nuts and dried fruits, particularly raisins. I have also provided recipes for a few sweet drinks, which go very well with any spicy meal and may be served in place of dessert.

Desserts in this chapter are not difficult to make and were chosen because the ingredients are readily available. They can be prepared beforehand, refrigerated, and frozen.

SOOJI KA HALVA

SEMOLINA DESSERT

MAKES 8

Indian children love this halva.

2¼ cups (560 ml) water
½ cup + 2 T (155 ml) sugar
¼ t (1.25 ml) cardamom seeds, pounded
3 T (45 ml) oil
3 T (45 ml) unsalted butter
¾ cup (180 ml) semolina
¼ cup (60 ml) raisins
¼ cup (60 ml) slivered almonds
1 T (15 ml) finely slivered pistachio nuts

Place the water, sugar and cardamom in a saucepan and bring to a boil over medium heat. Turn heat to low and simmer for 2 minutes. Remove from heat and set aside.
Heat the oil and butter in a large, non-stick frying pan or wok over medium heat. Add the semolina and stir and sauté until the semolina turns a light golden colour (not brown). Add the raisins and almonds and stir for 30 seconds longer. While stirring continuously, gradually pour in the sugar mixture, reduce heat and continue to stir and cook the halva for 6–8 minutes or until it is thick and runs off the sides of the pan. Remove from heat.
Spread evenly in a shallow dish (such as a flan dish), sprinkle with pistachio nuts and let it cool for 10–15 minutes. Cut into squares or diamond shapes and serve hot, warm or at room temperature, but not chilled.

TIP

The halva can be refrigerated for 3–4 days. Warm it up in the microwave before serving.

GAJJAR KA HALVA

CARROT PUDDING

SERVES 8

This halva is a great favourite during the winter months and is often served at functions such as weddings.

5 cups (1.25 litres) milk
1 kg carrots, grated
1 t (5 ml) cardamom seeds, pounded
½ cup (125 ml) ricotta cheese, crumbled
3 T (45 ml) oil
4 T (60 ml) unsalted butter
3 T (45 ml) raisins
3 T (45 ml) slivered almonds
¾ cup (180 ml) sugar
a generous pinch grated nutmeg
1 T (15 ml) chopped almonds

Bring the milk to a boil in a suitable heavy-based pan over medium heat. Add the carrots and cardamom and bring to a boil again. Reduce heat and cook, stirring frequently, until no liquid remains. Stir in the ricotta cheese, oil and butter. Stir and cook for 5 minutes.

Add all the remaining ingredients except the chopped almonds and continue to stir and cook for another 10 minutes or until the halva starts to draw away from the sides of the pan. Remove from heat.

Arrange in a serving dish and garnish with the chopped almonds.

Hot halva served with a scoop of vanilla ice cream is absolutely delicious.

TIP

Gajjar ka halva stays fresh for weeks when refrigerated.

GAJJAR KA HALVA

KHEER

KHEER

RICE PUDDING

SERVES 8

½ cup (125 ml) basmati rice*
3½ cups (875 ml) water
1 x 410 g tin evaporated milk
1 x 397 g tin sweetened condensed milk
½ t (2.5 ml) cardamom seeds, pounded
a generous pinch grated nutmeg

½ cup (125 ml) seedless raisins
½ cup (125 ml) chopped almonds
½ cup (125 ml) chopped cashew nuts
1 T (15 ml) finely slivered pistachio nuts
1 T (15 ml) finely slivered almonds

Wash and drain the rice. Bring the water to a boil in a heavy pan over medium heat. Add the rice and bring to a boil again. Lower the heat and simmer for about 25–30 minutes or until the rice is very soft. Stir in all the remaining ingredients except for the slivered pistachio nuts and almonds, and stir and cook for 10–15 minutes longer or until it is thick and creamy. Remove from heat.

Pour into a dessert bowl and sprinkle with the slivered nuts.

Serve hot in winter and chilled in summer. It tastes just as good either way.

* If not available, use any other good-quality long-grain rice.

NARIAL BARFI

COCONUT FUDGE

SERVES 8

½ cup (125 ml) water
½ cup (125 ml) sugar
a few strands of saffron or a little yellow food colouring

¼ t (1.25 ml) ground cardamom
3 cups (750 ml) coconut cream powder
2 t (10 ml) finely slivered pistachio nuts
2 t (10 ml) finely slivered almonds

Bring the water to a boil in a saucepan over medium heat. Add the sugar, saffron and ground cardamom and bring to a boil again, stirring continuously, until the sugar is fully dissolved. Reduce the heat to low and simmer for 2 minutes. Add the coconut and mix well.

Remove from heat and spread evenly onto a greased flat dish. Sprinkle with the slivered nuts and press gently. Allow to cool. Cut into small squares and serve.

Can also be served with morning or afternoon tea or coffee.

SWEET DRINKS

Although we have four seasons in India, our hot summer is the longest, especially in the northern part of the country. Every household has its own favourite cold drinks, but for me there is no substitute for lassi, thandai or nimbu-pani. These drinks are nutritious as well as tasty and easy to prepare and, served chilled, are great thirst quenchers on hot summer days. They are popular menu items in good Indian restaurants as well. Feel free to increase or reduce the liquid ingredients to get the consistency to your liking.

MEETHI LASSI
SWEET YOGHURT SHAKE
SERVES 4

4 cups (1 litre) low-fat yoghurt
4 T (60 ml) sugar, or to taste
1½ cups (375 ml) chilled water
1½ cups (375 ml) crushed ice

Place all the ingredients in a blender and blend for about 1 minute until frothy. Pour into chilled glasses and serve.

VARIATIONS

For mango lassi replace the sugar with 1 cup (250 ml) of fresh ripe mango pulp and follow the same method.

Savoury lassi is equally popular in Indian homes. Omit the sugar and instead add salt to taste, ½ t (2.5 ml) pepper and 1 t (5 ml) ground cumin or to taste, and follow the same method. Add 1 T (15 ml) finely chopped fresh mint leaves, mix with a spoon and pour into chilled glasses.

THANDAI
POPPY SEED AND ALMOND COOLER
SERVES 2

This is a very nutritious drink, full of protein, calcium, essential fatty acids and other vitamins and minerals.

½ cup (125 ml) ground almonds
4 t (20 ml) poppy seeds
1 T (15 ml) melon seeds (any variety)
8 whole peppercorns
2 cups (500 ml) skim milk (or low-fat)
4 t (20 ml) sugar, or to taste
1½ cups (375 ml) crushed ice

Place the ground almonds, poppy seeds, melon seeds and peppercorns in a bowl and add 1 cup (250 ml) of milk. Let it stand for 15 minutes. Pour this mixture into a blender and add the remaining milk and sugar. Blend until smooth and creamy. Add the ice and blend for 25–30 seconds longer. Pour into chilled glasses and serve.

MANGO LASSI

MASALE WALI CHAI

NIMBU PANI

NIMBU PANI

FRESH LIME OR LEMON JUICE

SERVES 2

2 cups (500 ml) water
2 T (30 ml) sugar, or to taste
3 T (45 ml) fresh lime or lemon juice
2 cups (500 ml) crushed ice
2 lemon slices or wedges, for garnish

Mix the water and sugar and stir until the sugar is fully dissolved. Add the remaining ingredients and mix. Serve in chilled glasses garnished with a slice or wedge of lime or lemon.

MASALE WALI CHAI

CHILLED SPICED TEA

SERVES 4

5 cups (1.25 litres) water
4 cardamom pods, cracked
6 whole cloves
1 x 3 cm piece stick cinnamon
2 t (10 ml) tea leaves (unflavoured)
4 T (60 ml) sugar, or to taste
¼ cup (60 ml) fresh lemon juice
2 cups (500 ml) crushed ice
fresh mint sprigs, for garnish

Pour the water into a saucepan and bring to a boil over medium heat. Add the whole spices and lower the heat. Cover and simmer for 5 minutes. Turn off the heat, add the tea leaves and sugar and cover again. Let the mixture stand for another 5 minutes. Stir well until the sugar is fully dissolved. Strain into a jug, discard the spices and tea leaves and let it cool. Add the lemon juice and crushed ice, and refrigerate until required. Serve in chilled glasses garnished with sprigs of fresh mint.

Because so many Indians are vegetarian — although a small percentage may occasionally

include eggs or fish in their meal plan — it is a challenging task to provide sufficient, high-quality

protein in a typical meal. To make food healthier and more nutritious, liberal use is made of milk

and milk products such as yoghurt and paneer (home-made cheese), as well as dried beans,

pulses and soya bean products.

BASIC
RECIPES

DAHI (yoghurt/curds)

Yoghurt, as everybody knows, is milk fermented with a friendly bacterial culture and has a slightly sour taste. It can be made with whole milk, low-fat or skim milk. The nutritive value of yoghurt is very similar to that of milk. It is rich in high-quality protein, calcium, phosphorus, riboflavin and other B vitamins and fat-soluble vitamins. Those who suffer from lactose (milk sugar) intolerance are often able to tolerate yoghurt better.

Naturally fermented yoghurt or dahi has been a staple food of Indians from the earliest times. No Indian meal is considered complete without a dish of yoghurt. It is also a very important ingredient in the preparation of numerous dishes, such as marinades for tandoori and other specialities, for thickening gravy, and to enhance flavour and texture in rice pulao.

Though commercial yoghurt is readily available in Indian cities, most people prefer to make their own fresh yoghurt at home, and indeed this is a daily ritual in most homes. Here in Johannesburg, I still make yoghurt at home every day. I used natural Greek yoghurt to begin with and it worked very well, and each batch now provides the starter culture for the following one. Once you are used to the taste and texture of fresh, natural yoghurt, you will not willingly compromise with commercial products. If kilojoules are a consideration, choose low-fat or non-fat yoghurt or milk.

DAHI
HOME-MADE YOGHURT
MAKES 4 CUPS (1 LITRE)

4 cups (1 litre) low-fat milk
3 T (45 ml) fresh natural yoghurt

Bring the milk to a boil. Lower the heat and allow to simmer for 5–7 minutes. Remove from heat and allow to cool until your finger can be kept immersed in it without discomfort. Place the yoghurt in a suitable bowl and add 2–3 T (30–45 ml) of warm milk to it. Mix well and then add this to the rest of the warm milk. Whisk thoroughly. Pour into a suitable bowl, cover and keep in a warm place to set for 6–8 hours, or preferably overnight. After it is set, refrigerate until required.

TIP
In winter it is advisable to use extra culture, wrap it in a tea towel and leave it in a warm place to set.

PANEER (Home-made cheese)

Paneer is another very important ingredient in Indian cooking and contains all the nutrients present in milk and yoghurt. It is made by coagulating or curdling milk with lemon juice, vinegar or with natural curds. Whey is then drained off and the solids are cut into cubes. These are used for making delicious and nutritionally rich dishes, especially good for vegetarians.

Paneer is often eaten in combination with pulses and lentils to enhance the protein value of a pure vegetarian meal. I have provided many recipes using paneer in combination with peppers, peas, chickpeas, spinach and so on. Paneer kebabs cooked over a braai or grilled, are mouth-watering.

Though full-cream milk makes the best paneer, I use low-fat milk with satisfying results. I prepare a whole lot of paneer at one time, divide it into smaller portions, place each portion in a freezer bag and freeze it. It stays fresh for months.

In South Africa there is no substitute for paneer available. Glancing at the recipe, you might feel it is too much trouble to prepare, but believe me it is not so. Try it once and it will soon become second nature.

PANEER
HOME-MADE CHEESE
MAKES 240 G

8 cups (2 litres) full-cream milk or 24 cups (6 litres)
   low-fat milk (see Tip below)
4 T (60 ml) fresh lemon juice

Bring the milk to a boil over high heat. Reduce heat to low and stir in the lemon juice. As soon as the milk is curdled and the solids are separate from the liquid whey, remove from heat. Pour the curdled mixture into a large sieve lined with muslin cloth. Let it drain without disturbing until the muslin is cold enough to handle.

Tie the muslin loosely and place on a chopping board. Set another board or a flat lid on top of the paneer. Place a heavy weight (such as a large cooking pot filled with water) on top. Allow to drain for 4–6 hours or until the paneer is firm and compact. Cut into cubes or as specified in the recipe. Frozen paneer stays fresh for months.

TIP
A litre of full-cream milk will yield approximately 120 g of paneer, whereas low-fat milk will yield only about 80 g. Paneer made with full-cream milk is softer and creamier than that made with low-fat milk.

SOYA BEAN PRODUCTS

Soya bean textured vegetable protein (TVP) products are the world's most efficient source of vegetable protein. Granules and chunks are made from high-quality, de-fatted soya flour.

They are easy to digest and contain almost 55% protein on a moisture-free basis as well as all the essential amino acids required for human nutrition. They also contain significant quantities of calcium and magnesium (essential for strong bones), along with B-group vitamins, vitamins E and K, and iron. Being low in fat, they are especially beneficial for keeping cholesterol in check and for cardiac and diabetic patients. They are extremely beneficial for vegetarians, who should include them in their daily food plan more frequently. Growing children and pregnant and nursing women would also benefit from the inclusion of soya products in their diet.

Soya products are almost neutral in taste, and as such can be added to any dish, sweet or savoury. They can be added to meat dishes to increase the quantity of the dish and to reduce saturated fat content. Soya is also a much more economical option than other proteins such as meat, milk and eggs.

PREPARING DRY SOYA PRODUCTS

Follow the instructions on the label, if there are any, or soak the granules or chunks for 10–15 minutes in enough hot water to swell the granules to almost three times their dry volume and the chunks to about double their dry volume. Squeeze and wash them with fresh water 2–3 times, squeeze out the water and discard it. The granules or chunks are now ready for use.

TOFU (Soya bean paneer or bean curd)

We associate tofu with paneer because of its texture and appearance. It is high in protein, and a rich source of calcium and other minerals and vitamins.

Tofu is low in saturated fats and has no cholesterol at all. It is also low in kilojoules compared with eggs and meat, and is an ideal food for the weight-conscious. As more and more people are becoming vegetarian, tofu and other soya products are increasingly being used.

Tofu is readily available at supermarkets or from oriental speciality stores. It is a very versatile product and can be used for making various delicious Indian dishes. Tofu can also be easily frozen for a long time, although its texture becomes a little chewy.

SOYA CHUNKS

SOYA GRANULES

TOFU

TANDOORI MASALA

MAKES ABOUT 1½ CUPS (375 ML)

This is used in all tandoori preparations and a few other dishes.

1 cup (250 ml) cumin seeds
½ cup (125 ml) coriander seeds
2 t (10 ml) fenugreek seeds*
½ t (2.5 ml) carum seeds*
8 green cardamom seeds, removed from pods
10 whole cloves
2 t (10 ml) whole black peppercorns
1 t (5 ml) ground mace
1 t (5 ml) fennel seeds
4 bay leaves
1 x 2 cm piece stick cinnamon

Grind all the spices to a fine powder. Store in an airtight jar and refrigerate. It will stay fresh for months.

*Though they impart a very distinctive aroma to tandoori preparations, you may omit them if you still have not taken a trip to an Indian store!

TIP
Typically most tandoori dishes are a deep orange or reddish in appearance. This is achieved by adding food colouring at the time of marinating. Personally I prefer not to use artificial colouring, but you may wish to. If so, combine a few drops each of red and yellow food colour for a bright orange tandoori colour.

GARAM MASALA

MAKES ABOUT 2 CUPS (500 ML)

1¼ cups (310 ml) cumin seeds
¾ cup (180 ml) coriander seeds
2 t (10 ml) green cardamom seeds
2 t (10 ml) black cardamom seeds*
1 T (15 ml) whole cloves
2 x 3 cm pieces stick cinnamon
2 T (30 ml) whole black peppercorns or to taste
4–5 bay leaves
⅛ nutmeg kernel

Grind all the spices to a fine powder. Store in an airtight jar and refrigerate. It stays fresh for months.

*If not available, use green cardamom seeds instead (i.e. 4 t (20 ml) green cardamom seeds).

TIP
You can add this to almost any dish, especially meat dishes with gravy. It has a very strong flavour, however, and should be used sparingly.

ROASTED GROUND CUMIN

I use this in many dishes because of its wonderful aroma. It is especially good in yoghurt side dishes and is so easy to prepare.

2–3 T (30–45 ml) cumin seeds

Roast the cumin seeds in a small frying pan without any oil until they turn dark brown. Allow them to cool, then grind them into a fine powder in a coffee grinder. Store in an airtight container.

ALMOND AND CASHEW NUT PASTE

Although nuts like almonds, pistachios and cashews are mostly used in Indian desserts and sweetmeats, they are sometimes used in savoury preparations to enhance the taste and texture. Keep a small stock of nuts handy or just buy them as needed.

I have used almond and cashew paste in many recipes in this book. These do not seem to be available at any supermarket or Indian store, and I therefore grind the paste myself. Just soak the nuts in water for a while and process in a food processor. Use fresh or prepare extra and freeze in small plastic bags for convenience.

PUDINA CHUTNEY
MINT CHUTNEY
MAKES ABOUT ¾ CUP (180 ML)

2 cups (500 ml) packed mint leaves, washed
¼ cup (60 ml) fresh coriander leaves, washed
1 small onion, coarsely chopped
2 t (10 ml) chopped root ginger
1 t (5 ml) chopped garlic
1 T (15 ml) lemon or lime juice (or to taste)
2 green chillies (optional)
1½ t (7.5 ml) ground cumin
2 t (10 ml) sugar (optional)
salt to taste

Place all the ingredients in a blender and blend until smooth. Remove to a bowl and adjust the seasoning according to taste. Tastes best when fresh. Store in a jar and refrigerate. It stays fresh for up to a week.

VARIATION
1 small raw mango (if in season) may be substituted for the lemon or lime juice. Peel the mango, discard the stone and blend it with the other ingredients.

DAHI PUDINA CHUTNEY
YOGHURT MINT CHUTNEY
MAKES ABOUT 1¾ CUPS (430 ML)

1 quantity pudina chutney (see recipe alongside)
1 cup (250 ml) low-fat yoghurt, hand-beaten
1 T (15 ml) lime juice
½ t (2.5 ml) pepper
½ t (2.5 ml) chilli powder
2 t (10 ml) sugar
salt to taste

Place all the ingredients in a bowl and mix well. Adjust seasoning. Chill and use fresh.

SERVING SUGGESTIONS
Serve with all tandoori dishes, such as murgi ka tikka and boti kabab, and some starters, such as chana bhajia or sabzi pakora.

Serve as a dip with potato wafers or tortillas.

GLOSSARY
OF HERBS AND SPICES

Indian names are in italics

The following herbs and spices are referred to in many of the recipes in this book. The majority of them are readily available at supermarkets, while some of them, marked with an *, may have to be purchased from a specialist Indian store in your city – see a suggested list of stockists on p 126.

It is preferable to buy small quantities of spices at a time and store them in airtight containers in a cool place or in the refrigerator, where they will stay fresh for months.

Bay leaf
Tej patta

Bay leaf is an aromatic herb used in many Indian meat dishes, rice pulao and biryani. It can be purchased in dried leaf or in powder form.

Black peppercorn
Kali mirch

Black peppercorns have a distinctive, pleasant flavour and are mildly pungent in taste. They are used whole in some preparations, otherwise in powder form, freshly ground, if at all possible.

Black salt*
Kala namak

This is not really black in colour as the name suggests but closer to deep purple. It has a strong, unusual flavour and tastes excellent in yoghurt dishes, raita and savoury snacks. All Indian provision stores carry it. It is preferably bought in powder form.

Cardamom – green and brown*
Choti elichi and kali elichi

Cardamom comprises dried, small green pods or large dark brown pods, with aromatic seeds inside. The seeds are used in meat and poultry dishes, rice pulao or biryani and for flavouring desserts. Cardamom is also used for making masala chai tea with aromatic spices and garam masala. It is available as whole pods, seeds or powder.

Carum seeds*
Ajwain

These very tiny, light-brown seeds have a flavour similar to that of thyme but are very bitter. Carum is an important ingredient in tandoori barbecue, masala and some Indian breads. It is available at Indian provision stores.

Chilli powder
Lal mirchi powder

Often extremely pungent and fiery, chilli powder's heat varies according to the variety. It should be used with caution and the quantity adjusted to taste. Cayenne pepper or paprika can be used as an alternative.

Cinnamon
Dalchini

Available in powder form or as bark, cinnamon is sweet and aromatic. It is used in rice preparations, some meat dishes and for making garam masala.

Cloves, whole
Long

Like cinnamon, cloves have a sweet aroma but are bitter to the taste. They are used in many savoury dishes and for making garam masala.

Coriander, fresh
Hara dhania

Better known as cilantro in the western world, this herb has a lovely fragrance. It is extensively used in cooking, for making delicious chutneys and dips, and for garnishing.

Coriander seeds
Sabat dhania

These aromatic seeds are used either coarsely ground or in powder form. They are an important ingredient in masalas and vegetable dishes.

Cumin
Zeera

These small, oval-shaped, light-brown seeds have small ridges and resemble caraway seeds. They are strongly aromatic and are readily available whole or in powder form.

Fennel seeds
Saunf

Fennel seeds are long, small and rice-like in shape and green in colour with a pleasant, sweetish fragrance. They're used as flavour enhancers and also as a mouth freshener after meals.

Fenugreek*
Methi seeds

An important and commonly used spice in India, Greece and Egypt. Fenugreek has small, hard seeds, brownish yellow in colour. They have a strong aroma when used in cooking, are slightly bitter in taste and excellent in tandoori masala and other dishes.

Garlic
Lahsun

Raw garlic has a strong, unpleasant flavour but cooking enhances its flavour and it is indispensable in most north Indian dishes, especially meat.

Ginger root
Adrak

Essential for various Indian recipes, it provides a distinctive flavour to meat and some vegetable dishes. Choose golden brown, fresh-looking ginger

root. If stored in an airtight container and refrigerated, it will stay fresh for several days. It can also be frozen.

Mace
Javitri

Used for many Indian meat dishes, mace is a web-like, brownish red aril that surrounds the kernel of nutmeg. It has a distinctive flavour and is not as strong as nutmeg.

Nutmeg
Jaifal

Nutmeg has a subtle, sweet flavour, used in savoury and sweet dishes.

Saffron
Kesar

Probably the most expensive spice, it is available in dried strands, has a slightly bitter, distinctive flavour and gives a pleasing yellow colour to food. Saffron is much used in northern India for savoury and sweet dishes.

Turmeric
Haldi

Available in powder form, is aromatic and slightly bitter in taste. Used in most Indian dishes for colour and flavour.

LIST
OF INDIAN SHOPS

Cape Town

Atlas Trading

94 Wale Street

Cape Town

Tel (021) 423 4361

Fax (021) 426 1929

Datar Spice Centre

31 Ernest Road

Rylands

Tel (021) 637 4203

Fax (021) 637 6250

Fargo Trading

Malta House

Malta Road

Salt River

Tel (021) 447 6620

Fax (021) 448 5048

Hotspice

Corner Reen and Carrick Street

Athlone Industria 1

Tel (021) 638 3132

Fax (021) 637 6862

Spice City

Johnston Road

Rylands Estate

Tel & Fax (021) 638 5118

Durban

Gorima's Spice Shop

110 A Musgrave Centre

Berea

Tel (031) 202 3882

Gorima's Spice Shop

11 A The Workshop

Durban

Tel (031) 304 0990

Gorima's Spice Shop

The Pavilion

Westville

Tel (031) 265 0099

Spice Emporium

31 Pine Street

Durban

Tel (031) 332 6662

Spice Paradise

Pride of Durban Spices

66 Nortcoast Road

Briardene

Tel (031) 564 8522

Gauteng

Aroma Spices

11 Sydenham Road

(near Rainbow Cash & Carry)

Fordsburg

Tel (011) 833 7888

Kwality Spice Works

28a Crown Road

Fordsburg

Tel (011) 834 2485

Laxmi Supermarket

4 Concord Place

Rose Avenue

Lenasia

Tel (011) 854 1355

S. Jivan Supermarket

393 Boom Street

Pretoria

Tel (012) 326 0722

INDEX